mLearning: Mobile Learning and Performance in the Palm of Your Hand

David S. Metcalf II, Ph.D.
Institute for Simulation and Training
University of Central Florida

with

John M. De Marco, President
John M. De Marco Communications

HRD Press, Inc. • Amherst • Massachusetts

Published by: HRD Press, Inc.
22 Amherst Road
Amherst, MA 01002
800-822-2801 (U.S. and Canada)
413-253-3488
413-253-3490 (fax)
www.hrdpress.com

ISBN 0-87425-906-1

Table of Contents

Acknowledgments ix

Chapter One: Introduction 1

Chapter Two: Wireless Overview 7
- Review of PDA Technologies 7
- Review of Smart Phones 10
- Types of Wireless Connections 12
- Conclusion 18

Chapter Three: mLearning Value Proposition 19
- When to Use Wireless 22

Chapter Four: Case Studies—Sales 29
- Introduction 29
- Vodafone Academy WAP Performance Modules 29
- 3COM® University Uses the Palm™ for Mobile Learning 34
- Conclusion 38

Chapter Five: Case Studies—Services 39
- Wireless e-Learning IP Troubleshooting Field Guide for the Palm VII 39
- Smart Phones 45
- Valero's Mobile Procedure Access 46
- Real-Time and Work Flow-Based Learning in the U.S. Defense Industry 48

Chapter Six: Case Studies—Business Processes and Performance 53
- Introduction 53
- ALLTELL 53
- Communication Tools 60
- Sales Campaign 61
- Implementation and Challenges 61

Measurement/Evaluation of Outcomes 64
QUALCOM, Inc. 68
Nokia Quality WAP Modules for Methods and Tools 77
Unilever mLearning 78

Chapter Seven: Instructional Design Principles for Wireless Development 81
Introduction to ISD Innovations for mLearning 81
Anecdotes from the Field 81
Instructional Development Shifts 84
User interface Shifts 85
Learner Experience Shifts 85
Details of the Instructional Design Model for mLearning and Wireless Performance Support.... 86
Details of the Instructional Design Process for mLearning 87
Constructivism 88
Concept Map of a Balanced Diet 90
Collaborative Learning 91
Instant Information Access 92
Conclusion 93

Chapter Eight: Multimedia Development for Mobile 95
Introduction 95
Principles 95
Capabilities and Current Limitations 96
Development 100
HTML 100
WAP 101
Authoring Tools 101
Specialized Platform Tools and Software Development Kits (SDKs) 103
Delivery 106

Vector Graphics 109
Conclusion 109

Chapter Nine: The Integration of Wireless Learning and Performance Support into Other Core Function Wireless Initiatives 111
Introduction 111
Links to CRM (Customer Relationship Management) 111
Siebel and Oracle 113
SimplexGrinnell and Valero Energy 114
Mobile Augmented Reality: Symbol University Handheld Learning Assistant 115
Conclusion 123

Chapter Ten: Other Options for Mobile Professionals 125
Synchronization 125
Voice-based Access 128

Chapter Eleven: mLearning Implications for Next Generation Technologies 131
Collaboration 131
The Convergence of Voice, Data, and Motion Images 133
eBooks: Electronic Classroom Surrounds Using Wireless Technologies 135
Applications to eLearning 137
Future Innovations in eBooks 138
Handtop Computing 139
Wearable Computers 140
iPods 141
Transcoders—LCMSs with Transcoding Functions 143

Blogs, Audio Blogs, and the Future of Online Journaling 144
Mobile Gaming 145
Innovative Programs and Projects Academic ADL Co-Lab 150
MOBIlearn Project 152
Conclusion 154

References 155

Acknowledgments

I want to start off by acknowledging this spark of interest that happened in the mid-1990s with the launch of the first Palm Pilot, for both my colleagues and team members at NASA's Kennedy Space Center, where we first started to explore the idea of mobile learning on handheld devices.

Next, I'd like to thank colleagues and team members from RWD Technologies, where we did some of the first commercial implementations of mobile learning, including award-winning initiatives, many of which you will see highlighted in this book. And most recently, I would like to acknowledge the collaboration and partnership of the University of Central Florida's Institute for Simulation and Training.

None of this would be possible without the friendship and support of Dr. Larry Bielawski. His invaluable mentoring in the writing process and our ongoing collaboration has been a true blessing.

I would also like to thank John M. De Marco for his editing and compilation of this volume and the invaluable time helping organize and edit this content developed through mobile processes. Also invaluable in this process was Linda Mikell, with support for transcription and tight deadlines to meet. Thanks to Lisa Upham for final edits and reference checks.

On a personal note, I would like to thank my family for their ongoing support: my parents and everyone else who suffered through long hours of additional work, review of drafts, and what could be maddening conversation about a topic that I am very passionate about. My loving wife Katy and my wonderful son Adam have supported me through all of this. Thank you for your support.

Most importantly, I thank my Lord Jesus Christ for inspiring innovation and allowing me to explore new frontiers.

Chapter One:
Introduction

Imagine yourself stuck in a busy airport chock full of business commuters, watching delay after delay post to the digital screen that announces incoming and departing flights. You have your e-ticket confirmation in one hand and a handheld device in the other. Rather than allowing your time to be completely wasted by circumstances beyond your control, you are absorbing some continuing education—with posted learning materials, or better yet a live instructor from hundreds if not thousands of miles away.

What if, in the not-too-distant future, you could gain back hours of such useful time each day. How can this be possible?

Considering the growing trends of mobility in our society, it's easy to see that gaining back some of the time we spend on the road, in airports, and even waiting in lines could be a great source of productivity. According to a 2002 study by Texas A&M University's Transportation Institute, the average U.S. commute to work is more than 25 minutes. Multiply that by two, and you have a significant amount of time that people commute and travel to work every single day (Schrank & Lomax, 2002).

Capturing even a fraction of this time back for other activities would be a significant improvement in not only each person's individual productivity, but also in national productivity for any country that decides to capitalize on existing and emerging trends of mobility. Such trends are strongly linked to the concept of the individual as a life-long learner and organizational performance, prompting us to explore in-depth areas of mobile learning, or "mLearning" for short.

mLearning combines the technologies of mobile communications with "eLearning," which, for the purpose of this discussion, we can define as any form of electronically delivered learning material with an emphasis on Internet-based technologies (Brown, 2005). It allows you to have connective, online access even while you are on the go in a mobile setting—vitally important for a large portion of professionals in our midst. Realizing that "courses in a box" are not always very productive or user friendly, the goal of mLearning is to develop learning content that integrates with mobile applications and provides learning and performance in a just-in-time, just-in-place dynamic.

This researcher is excited to present some opportunities to look at ways that learning and performance support (just-in-time learning) can be enhanced by the use of late-breaking technologies. These include: mobile and handheld communications; audio and multimedia that can be delivered while driving; technologies for accessing enterprise systems while on the go; electronic books, reference materials, and small courses; and many other learning interventions being placed in formats that can be delivered via mobile devices or through methods and techniques that allow you to use them while on the go.

Many if not most of you reading this book have a device nearby such as a personal digital assistant (PDA) or smart phone. Chances are some of you use them to surf the Internet, check e-mail, and schedule events. These same devices are rapidly becoming mobile "classrooms" that transcend any brick-and-mortar setting.

Furthermore, it is entirely plausible that some of you may immediately be thinking, "Well, this is not that new of an idea; I have seen examples of course materials and educational resources delivered on handhelds for years." And perhaps you are even pondering, "If you are going to tell me that you are going to squeeze every little course that you have into some little box and expect to have your users love it and be as enthralled with it as you were upon creating it, think again!"

This is true! However, the most interesting thing about our era is that we are seeing a surge in the capability, connectedness, and cost-effectiveness of eLearning technologies. Another key premise of this book, which will be repeatedly emphasized, is that most people do not want to pour through course materials while hunched over a very small screen—but are willing to get the right information at just the right time, just about anywhere, especially during the dull lull of waiting for a plane, train, or any other service with a queue.

The more you can integrate those learning functions that you use most often, the better off you are—and the more effective the teacher who is trying to reach the students. Personal and work-related productivity can seamlessly tie together, blurring the imaginary line located between the two.

"Between those who search aggressively for opportunities to learn more about IT (Information Technology) and those who choose not to learn anything at all, there are many who recognize the potential value for their everyday lives and who realize that a better understanding will be beneficial to all," says Marius Kemp (2005) of Damelin International College. "Information technology has entered our lives over a relatively brief period of time with little warning and essentially no formal educational preparation for most people. Many who currently use information technology have only a limited understanding of the tools they use and a (probably correct) belief that they are under-utilizing them" (Kemp, 2005).

This book seeks to increase such awareness, for the benefit of all. We will emphasize performance orientation, rather than a pure learning orientation like more traditional courseware. We will shine the spotlight on learning that interfaces with your lifestyle and work style, making things more efficient for you rather than adding more to your plate.

The following is a diagram showing the orientation of wireless technology in relationship to performance support and a blended eLearning model.

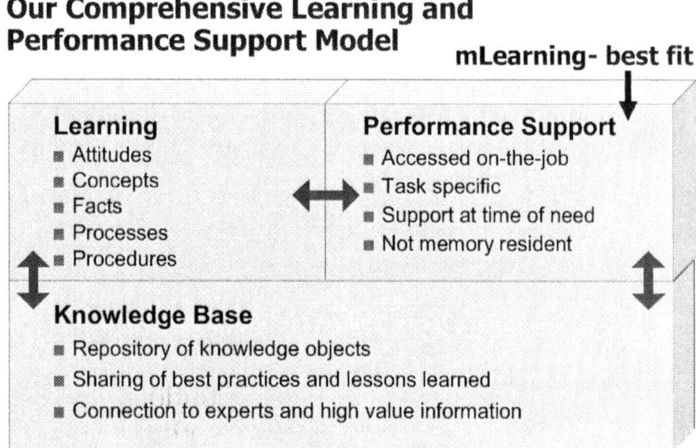

However, before delving too deeply into learning theory and function, let us step back and gain some clarity on some of the core wireless and mobile technologies that are reshaping communication and information delivery, and enabling mLearning.

Chapter Two will feature an overview of devices and network terminology that will clear up mobile jargon. You will also get a snapshot of wireless technologies and trends, including PDAs and smart phones.

In Chapter Three, we will examine how these emerging technologies facilitate those "stolen moments of learning" that help us to more seamlessly tie working and learning together. A primary focus here will be a deeper understanding on how mobile learning factors into performance and productivity.

This will be followed by three chapters of case studies, looking at the advantages of mLearning in various settings that include sales, services, and personnel or operational examples, respectively.

In Chapter Seven, we will discuss key practices and learning theories related to wireless design and development. This includes learning theories, design models, and best practices in instructional design for mLearning.

Chapter Eight examines how multimedia has developed in the wireless world. Understanding the tools for development and delivery will help you make smart choices about when to use multimedia and what tools are currently available.

In Chapter Nine, we will look at core wireless functions such as customer relationship management (CRM) software, and how mLearning can be integrated with these core business functions that are driving mobile technology use.

Chapter Ten takes us beyond wireless data to see how synchronization and voice-based mobile functions can be used in mLearning. And our final section, Chapter Eleven, examines next generation technologies such as ebooks, handtops, iPods, and wearables.

Throughout our review of trends, instructional models, media, technologies, case studies, and future innovations, we will explore a performance-driven approach to the emerging discipline of mLearning. Enjoy!

Chapter Two:
Wireless Overview

So why look at mobile, handheld, and wireless technologies at all? What do they have to do with learning?

Let's review a few key trends. In 2005, the year of this writing, The Gartner Group expects wireless headsets to reach one billion units in circulation, outnumbering televisions and personal computers combined. Gartner also estimates that more than 75 million handheld PDAs are now in use (Gartner, 2005).

This impressive surge in the use of such technologies necessitates an overview of the various types of PDAs that are on the market.

Review of PDA Technologies

Thanks to scheduling and contact management functions, the PDA has been highly successful and has a significant installed user base in both the United States and abroad. This indispensable business tool is rapidly expanding its capability in terms of reduced size, increasing battery life, multimedia functions, and special purpose applications (such as barcode reading, credit card transactions, and most importantly, wireless/mobile Internet access).

Currently, PDAs fall into three primary camps with several emerging offshoots. The Palm OS (Operating System), Windows Pocket PC OS, and the two-way, pager-based PDAs (RIM Blackberry and Motorola series devices) make up the bulk of the marketplace. Let's examine each in more detail.

PalmOne

The Palm OS commands the largest share of the market (currently around 65 percent worldwide) and encompasses a wide range of special purpose devices from companies such as Palm, IBM, Sony, TRG, Symbol and Handspring, among others. Palm also has a large network—65,000-plus—of Palm software developers. The operating system and devices have simplicity of use, ease of integration, and specialization as key advantages.

Processor speed is a key issue to be addressed if more functionality is desired. Some devices have added special functions such as audio players, digital cameras, cell phones, or credit card readers as examples of integrated functions. The devices have extended far beyond merely serving as personal information managers (PIMs). Sporting a sizable installed base and expanding functions, it is clear to see how delivery of short segments of learning could be a valuable addition to the existing handheld uses.

Pocket PC

The Pocket PC platform from Microsoft is the latest iteration in a series of devices based on a "light" version of Microsoft Windows. The functions are similar to Windows and are tightly integrated. Numerous formats such as Word, Excel, and Web and e-mail functions are available without conversion from a desktop machine to the Pocket PC. Some of the most striking features about these devices are the rich multimedia functions, including advanced graphic support, animation, audio, and even video.

The Windows operating system is also being ported to cell phones and hybrid PDA/phone devices, and is being called Stinger for Microsoft Smartphones. Once battery life is increased, price points drop slightly, and a critical mass of developers is reached, these devices will be commonplace.

Most recently, Microsoft has released the Mobile 5 version of their operating system. New features open up even greater capability and device flexibility similar to the Palm: the devices and OS are expandable to include many specialized functions such as high-speed wireless cards, digital cameras, micro drives that can store movie libraries, and external presentation/projector managers. All of these specialized functions and multimedia capabilities make rich media eLearning a distinct option on these devices.

Two-Way Pagers

The lion's share of the two-way pager market belongs to Motorola and RIM. Each has devices that have expanded beyond simple messaging systems to take on PDA functions such as PIMs, larger screens, mini-keyboards, and most recently e-mail and Web access. These devices are part of systems that have great coverage throughout the United States and boast long battery life (weeks instead of hours or days). Most importantly, they provide instant, live access to facilitate real-time information. For timely data, or message-based learning delivery models, this platform holds significant potential. The RIM Blackberry is pulling ahead in this category and has added full cellular access to many of their latest devices.

Review of Smart Phones

Smart phones are data-enabled cellular phones. This broad category spans everything from simple text messaging, to phones that expand open and provide full PDA, Web, and e-mail functions, along with standard voice operations and simple text messaging.

Nokia 9500 Communicator

PalmOne Treo 650

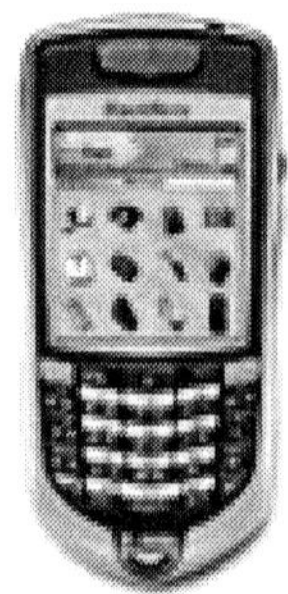

Blackberry 7100t

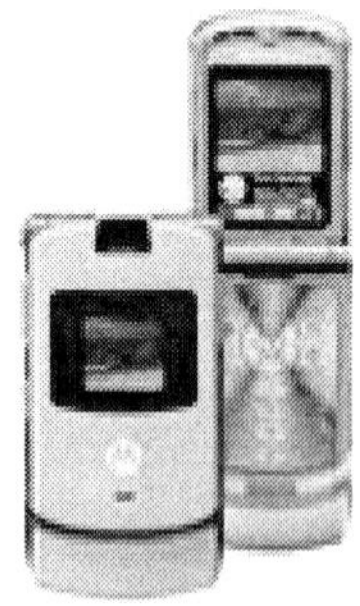

Moto Razr V3

There are many smart phone vendors, including Nokia, Motorola, SonyEricsson, Mitsubishi, Audiovox, LG,

Kyocera, Panasonic, Siemens, and Samsung. Most of the devices currently feature simplified Web access through a specially designed format called Wireless Application Protocol (WAP). Similar to the HTTP Web protocol, WAP can deliver data directly to the small screen on the cell phone.

The widespread use of cell phones—topping one billion worldwide—opens up a large market for this model, which offers quick, small morsels of learning, exactly when needed and in any location. Most of these cellular phones have a light operating system, but some are beginning to provide additional functions and require an operating system such as the popular European Symbian OS for cell phones and a select set of PDAs. Smart phones have short messaging (SMS) capability, which often is referred to as "texting" for sending short notes, much like instant messaging.

This communication function for connecting students and instructors or expert networks represents a broad, untapped functionality for informal learning networks. Additionally, some wireless network carriers are starting to offer location-based services that can be used to send context-sensitive information based on location.

The most exciting aspect of the smart phones is the potential impact of upgrades to high-speed data transfer. We will examine the particulars of this in our next section, but in a few years it will be possible to send broadband content (normally suitable for cable modems, high speed T-1 landlines, or DSL) across the cellular carrier networks. During a recent layover in Chicago, I had over 1.5 Mbps (T-1 speed) using my Bluetooth cell phone as a modem link on my computer (more on Bluetooth below). This will open up a world of opportunity for multimedia data to be delivered for a variety of purposes, including learning.

Types of Wireless Connections

WAN, MAN, LAN, PAN

Now that we've piqued your interest with devices and potential functions, let's take a step back and look at the networking technology that enables these devices. While there are whole books written on this subject, we will try to give you a quick snapshot so that you can begin thinking about what technologies are available. We will also attempt to demystify some of the common technologies and categories, beginning with the cryptic acronyms in the section title: WAN (Wide Area Network), MAN (Metropolitan Area Network), LAN (Local Area Network), and PAN (Personal Area Network). Let us categorize wireless technologies into these areas, which are roughly based on the breadth of geography they can cover.

WAN

WAN can be thought of as your cellular phone coverage with a national or international carrier. Devices in this category are smart phones, cellular devices, cellular modems, pager networks, the Internet backbone (in conjunction with local wireless access points), and even satellite systems.

The hottest topic in this area, as mentioned in the last section, is high-speed access through the latest generation cellular infrastructure. These are typically referred to by *x*G (1G, 2G, 2.5G, 3G, 4G). We are currently emerging into the 2.5G range in the United States, while some areas of Europe and Asia are already well into 3G technology deployment.

What does this mean? Specifically, 1G is the equivalent of older analog cellular technology. 2G is the equivalent of existing digital networks for voice only (typical data rates are 4.8 kilobits per second [kbps] to 14.4 kbps). Additionally, 2.5G is based on a technology called General Packet Radio Service (GPRS) and typically produces between 14.4 kbps and 60 kbps (with a theoretical maximum of 154 kbps). This is about the same as existing landline-based modems today. Furthermore, 3G, which will be based on technologies such as Universal Mobile Telecommunications System (UMTS) and other emerging standards, may produce between 80 kbps and 384 kbps with averages like those seen on Integrated Services Digital Network (ISDN) lines. Some say the range may be extended to 2 Mbps (equivalent to a T-1 high-speed or cable modem connection), but this will not be the norm for a while, although through Enhanced Data GSM Environment (EDGE) technology, these speeds can be seen in major metropolitan areas today.

In addition, some have begun to discuss 4G technology, which ranges from 2 Mbps through a possible 10 Mbps, but is rather distant at this point in time. However, all of this does show great long-term promise for devices that you can take anywhere in the country (or possibly the world).

Another WAN technology with emerging promise is satellite transmission. Currently, several providers have satellite phone networks in place and a few (such as DirectPC from Hughes and Tachyon) have high-speed (+400 kbps) service for Internet data transmission. As hardware and antennas shrink, it may be possible to deliver content to mobile devices across these networks as well.

Finally, several providers are exploring a higher speed, micro-cellular strategy (a shoebox-sized transceiver mounted on light posts and utility poles). Sierra Wireless has made wireless modems that operate at 128 kbps or higher and are connected to a laptop or handheld. The service has only been available in a handful of cities and airports. This strategy of microcellular devices is being promoted and explored by several carriers for application to handheld and wireless service.

MAN

Metropolitan Area Networks (MANs) can be more difficult to categorize than WANs or LANs. There are many technologies being rolled out to cover a region smaller than a country or geography, but larger than a single building or campus. These networks are often referred to as MANs, but there is much debate about where the LANs, MANs, and WANs start and stop. The core area we will examine are those technologies built for more than one building, but not encompassing a region larger than a city. A few key technologies fall into this area, including fixed wireless technology, lasers, and microcellular systems.

MAN technologies primarily bridge the gap between LAN and WAN technologies. Conversely, WAN and LAN technologies are increasing bandwidth and extending range respectively to cover the MAN area.

Fixed Wireless

Several types of fixed wireless exist. Some providers are using this technology to compete with cable operators to send cable television channels to a wireless receiver. This is also being used to send high-speed Internet data across a wireless connection at speeds similar to a cable modem or DSL line. LMDS (Local Multipoint Distribution Services) and MMDS (Multipoint Microwave Distribution System, or Multi-channel Multi-point Distribution System) are common acronyms for this type of fixed wireless transmission. In addition, some handheld technologies can take advantage of fixed wireless.

LAN

While many wireless LAN technologies exist, one stands out in today's market. WiFi, short for wireless fidelity, is a generic term that refers to any type of 802.11 network, whether 802.11b, 802.11a, dual-band, etc. It allows someone to connect to the Internet from any location without the need to plug into a wall, operating much like a cell phone. WiFi enables computers to send and receive data indoors and out, anywhere within the range of a base station, and operate several times faster than the quickest cable modem connection.

Within the context of mobility, there are many aspects of the local area network that come into play. Most particularly is what we would call a "campus setting," or a location within the confines of one particular work environment, office building, or area of operation. Understanding how local area networks can perform is another vital aspect to understanding how you can be mobile within a small area.

The most important aspect of understanding how the local area network affects wireless and, of course, mobile communications is how this will affect the learning. Most of you connect over cable modems or T-1 lines for your home-based connections that link you out to the Internet. These typically operate at the speed of 1.5 megabits per second (Mbps) as a typical example. 1.5 Mbps is still eight times slower than the WiFi, or 802.11B, 11 Mbps that many of you have in your local area networks. 802.11a operates at 54 Mbps and 802.11g allows a network to use both 11 Mbps and 54 Mbps wireless data transfer with greater security (802.11x). Too many numbers? Don't worry; much of this is seamless to users and developers at this point.

It's easy to see how mLearning might allow advanced media, like video and animations, to be delivered in a local setting, but might be a little bit more difficult to connect via some of the technologies we've discussed at the wide area network level (WAN). Understanding the unique characteristics on how much data can be delivered on each of these networks is vital to realizing how you will be able to use this from a technology design standpoint once you have your structural design committed.

Beginning with the end in mind though, it is important to understand how this technology, both opportunities and limitations, can affect the delivery of your information. It will also be important to understand this to know what your audience will be expecting and to know they will be able to accept in the way of mobile learning or mLearning.

PAN

Now that we've taken a look at the local area network, let's explore what happens just in your office space—or within the area of a small, tightly constrained domain, maybe feet from your person as you're traveling. This phenomenon has been dubbed a PAN, or a personal area network, and encompasses many of the tools in your office setting as well as devices that might need to interconnect while you're traveling. A good example is a cell phone, which can be connected by a Bluetooth technology to be able to send data, whether it's an address book or schedules or otherwise, between your phone and your laptop. Other examples might be the interconnection of using a cell phone as a modem via Bluetooth or infrared type communications back to a laptop, PDA, or even new handtop computers that we will explore further in other technology chapters.

It's even easier now through Bluetooth technology and infrared to connect PDAs with cell phones. Many of the latest generations of printers and scanners also have Bluetooth connectivity. All of these things start to create a wireless network that centers on your person and personal devices, and even has other peripherals like wireless headsets that can sit in someone's ear and allow them to access their cell phone, which might still be attached to their belt.

A world of opportunities start to open up with Bluetooth technology. It operates at intermediate speeds of 15 Mbps and is becoming increasingly more common in many devices—not just computers and cell phones, but in PDAs, printers, scanners, other biometric devices for scanning the identity of your finger tips or eye scanners, headsets, speaker phones, and a plethora of other devices that might be useful to you in your daily communications and exchange of information.

The personal area network is a growing phenomenon that is vital to the movement of learning to meet the needs and challenges of mobile communications and our growing society that is more and more on the move everyday.

IR and Laser

Almost as a side note to our discussion of wireless for handhelds is the possibility to transmit data with pulses of light or lasers. The ability to send data to handhelds via this communication medium is just beginning to be explored. The technology is also limited by environmental conditions and linear paths for transfer.

Conclusion

As we have seen, numerous wireless technologies, trends, and products are revolutionizing how we communicate and process valuable information at various locations and with varying degrees of power. Let us next turn our attention to how these emerging technologies offer us "stolen moments of learning" at just the right time.

Chapter Three:
mLearning Value Proposition

Perhaps you can relate to those "stolen moments" of learning when you are standing in line, flip open your Palm phone, and browse an e-newsletter or e-mail. Personal and work-related productivity can seamlessly tie together, blurring the imaginary line located between the two.

The aspect of having all pertinent information accessible to you at a given moment can lead to a "time rebate" of as much as one hour or longer per day. Imagine all the time you spend cruising down the halls, waiting for people to show up in between meetings, waiting for the next phone call, waiting for the e-mail, waiting for the document, plane, driver, train...waiting, waiting, waiting!

Mobile makes the most sense when seen in the context of amplifying personal productivity through a just-in-time, just-in-place dynamic, integrating the functions that persons use most often—a potential godsend in particular for those technicians who work in the field and for those persons patrolling the sales floors. While not always recognized, workplace support has the greatest impact on performance—and companies that provide support that is accessed on the job, task specific, available at time of need, and not dependent on memory will continue to thrive.

Addressing such dynamics, wireless and handheld technology is reshaping many industries, including eLearning, and many vendors are launching new products and services to capitalize on this important trend. Seeking to address their customers through a performance support perspective, vendors are designing mLearning products they can deliver to multiple formats in order to suit a diversity of needs and locations.

A February 2005 article in *Financial Times*, written by Chloe Veltman, notes that changes in work and training practices have played a role in the emergence of mLearning. The research company In-Stat/MDR estimated the number of "remote and mobile workers" in the United States to have reached approximately 94,000,0000 by the end of 2004, or nearly 40 percent of the workforce (In-Stat, 2005).

And yet, the article continues, it's not just about work. Ron Edwards, of the UK-based learning innovation consultancy Ambient Performance, says projects such as the Washington, D.C.-based initiative Serious Games are exploring and developing game-based learning tools. "The popularity of playing games on mobile devices including mobile phones lends itself very naturally to mLearning, and can bring fun and effectiveness to corporate training and communications," Edwards says in the *Financial Times* piece. "We expect to see more of this in the future."

At this point there may still be soft demand for these mobile offerings in terms of pure learning functions, but the potential is significant. Initial service offerings have just begun to scratch the surface. Content vendors such as Global Learning Systems, Global Knowledge, Learn2.com, and Isopia have offered an impressive array of mini-courses for either the Palm or the Pocket PC platform. In addition, infrastructure vendors such as Generation21, Isopia (now part of Sun Education), and SumTotal have all piloted wireless access to scheduling information, rosters, and other administrative features for training.

These two areas characterize the majority of eLearning offerings in the wireless space today. Small "courselets" and "scheduling access" represent a very logical migration to the wireless platform, but lack creativity in the application of features very unique to wireless content delivery.

As stated in this author's previous book, *Blended eLearning*, the shift from a training orientation to a performance support orientation is an important overall framework change. It is characterized by short learning segments that can be measured in seconds rather than hours, and may not follow the standard format of objective definition, content delivery, and assessment or practice.

The need defines the objective. How you develop your content and structure the learning experience is more important than the actual technology. Companies should design with the environment, content, learner, and technology in mind, and users should examine ways they can creatively weave a wireless delivery strategy into their training efforts.

These types of shifts in thinking and development must take place for us to truly unleash the power of wireless delivery for eLearning. A truly blended eLearning approach can take these devices to the next level of utility for individuals as well as organizations.

Understanding how to access corporate knowledge and use the tools effectively to improve on-the-job performance could be the "killer application" for wireless and round out the currently limited courseware capabilities of these devices.

When to Use Wireless

In this section, we will examine some of the ways that wireless is being used from both an audience and business function perspective. We will also explore some of the ways learning functions tie into these business opportunities. An integrated performance-based approach combines the best of both worlds of business process and learning function, and leads to performance even when people are on the go.

Business Function, Learning Function: An Integrative Performance Approach

There are three main categories of business function where we see mobile and wireless devices being used consistently and commonly. The first is the area of sales for the on-the-go salesperson. The second is in the area of service, where technicians are mobile and distributed to go and provide field support for a variety of products, services, and even internal initiatives. And third, as many of you know, the busy executive who is constantly on the move needs access to up-to-date information and resources. This is not only to control and monitor how the business is doing back on the home front, but to have access to information at his or her fingertips, right when and where it is needed. There are substantial productivity gains to be made in each of these different sections.

Sales

Within the area of sales performance, having access to product and services information is critical to the sales process. Time-to-competency and improved sales performance are often equated to the salesperson's knowledge of the product or service they are selling.

Having the details of products and services at your fingertips can greatly improve performance, especially in areas with a significant base of technical information that must be provided in a very specific way—and with 100 percent accuracy. This is vital in technical sales such as computers and networking, and is even more important in highly regulated areas and those involving medical and health issues.

A perfect example is the pharmaceutical industry. Pharmaceutical representatives live and die by the type of information they can provide to busy doctors. Garnering their attention by giving them education on new products, drug formulas, and protocols, and addressing questions that doctors and other healthcare providers might have is crucial to success in this area.

Having reviewed the sales process and how the role of sales professional can be improved with the use of mobile and wireless technologies, let's look at how service professionals can also benefit from these new technologies.

Service

Access to Customer Relationship Management (CRM) and Supply Chain Management (SCM) systems can be useful for the service technician, much in the same way as the information we reviewed with Valero Energy and their quality inspectors in the case studies chapters. The service technician who is providing field services for things like network equipment (as in the case of IP Trouble Shooting Guide) with detailed network information, along with the ability to order parts, benefits when work flow and performance support can be integrated to combine the best of business processes and the necessary service knowledge.

The service technician benefits in several ways with these mobile communication devices. First, having access to the same information that one would have back at their desk or their office is vital to solving and correcting problems as quickly as possible.

Another key benefit is the ability to have access to scheduling information, directions, and—particularly on some of the newest models of phones and PDAs—access to GPS information. The latter, also known as location awareness, tells where a service problem is, or where an address is that might need to be accessed so that there are fewer missed turns, missed directions, and wrong addresses that keep a service technician from getting to their service location as quickly and efficiently as possible. Understanding how to make the greatest use of "windshield time" (drive time) and to minimize it, is another area that has great implications of improvement for service technicians as well as the sales functions we looked at above.

Another area of benefit to service providers from a specific industry is in the automobile rental agency market. For many years, we've observed how check-in clerks have access to mobile devices with printers, bar code readers, and even credit card swipes. Sometimes, they even possess wireless terminal access packet information about each service and rental contract. A receipt can quickly be printed, a car can be checked in for re-servicing and reprovisioning, and the computer system can be updated—all in one convenient workflow process. Adding learning and learning improvement to this equation could get newer employees up to speed more quickly, and allow for specific service contracts to be understood more easily. This provisioning process is greatly enhanced with the use of mobile technology.

We are also seeing service providers in law enforcement, fire, and rescue, as well as other emergency and first responders, make significant use of mobile technology to speed up the processes that they go through in protecting and serving. This even addresses the arena of writing traffic citations, but oftentimes in the core function of such personnel, seconds are vital for people's health, safety, and well-being.

There are many examples of such increased efficiency recognized each year through the Excellence Awards sponsored by Mobile Enterprise Magazine and other wireless technology solution providers. Understanding how all areas of service can be greatly enhanced is something that will continue to grow over the course of time.

In later sections, we will look at some of the innovations being provided in the service area to cut down on windshield time, such as SimplexGrinnell's voice-based access to information portals and learning and performance.

Executives and Professionals

In this section, we will look at how busy executives and other professionals who are constantly on the move can get access to information they need.

Having access to the same information that's available back in the home office can be quite convenient. This starts with general information about contacts, scheduling, and other support group systems, but it extends much further than that. Having access to enterprise systems, details about direct reports and employees, and access to other reports and functions on how the business is running also is crucial. Many PDAs and smart phones and the standard laptops, as well as the emerging tablet and handheld market, are providing some of this critical information.

Busy executives are taking advantage of downtime in airports, waiting in line for services, and their daily commute by using these wireless devices. Understanding how to use these productivity enhancers is an area of research that Dr. Tom Davenport is exploring in great detail, with personal information and personal knowledge management a trend he has identified as a key driver in the information economy for knowledge workers across the globe. Making the most of this will be a trait of professionals, managers, and executives as we proceed through the 21st century.

A good example we touched on earlier with the pharmaceuticals rep is the doctor or other healthcare professional with whom they might be working. Imagine the scenario of being able to walk into the doctor's office and beam PDA to PDA, or PDA to Smart Phone, new formulary information or new action tables. It would be useful to the doctor to have this quick reference and be able to review it in more detail later. Doctors also have access to other information, such as the latest research from Medline, Epocrates, and other medical journals. They can further speed up their work flow processes by having patient charting and other detailed information about a particular patient available to them in a secure format, one that is mindful of recent regulations such as HIPAA (Health

Insurance Portability and Accountability Act) and other privacy concerns for healthcare information.

The ability to easily automate the process of sending scripts to pharmacies is another example of how this technology is being used. Doctors who are on the go in the hospital, private practice, or other medical facilities have access to their information—as well as the larger scope of information for diagnosis, treatment, and prognosis. No one individual is as smart as the collective professional populace, and having access to a broad base of information is great performance support; speeds up the work flow of a knowledge worker; and can lead to greater quality care, improved patient health and safety, and quicker processing with proper diagnosis.

In the legal profession, access to case law from one's own jurisdiction and others across the globe can be provided through Westlaw.com, LexisNexis, and other databases sporting both proprietary and public information. Tying these to scheduled items and cases, a lawyer is facing an integrated work flow of achieving performance right when and where it's needed.

This is another example, as we saw throughout this chapter, of how business processes are being reshaped through the use of mobile and wireless communication technologies. Because of the importance to our discussion of mLearning, we have demonstrated how these professional services are enhanced by the use of learning theory and performance support interventions.

Let us now examine three chapters worth of case studies that will take us deeper into what these areas can look like when implemented.

Chapter Four:
Case Studies—Sales

Introduction

Well, enough background, terminology, and strategies; let's look at some real-world examples of mLearning!

As mentioned previously, many organizations have attempted to shove courseware into a small mobile device and expected learners to stay focused on a 20-minute module. However, the nature and complexity of the information delivered versus screen real estate, along with the nature of attention spans, often make this impractical.

While there is some merit to this approach for reinforcement and learning of basic concepts, most of the examples to follow conform to the performance, support-oriented approach we have been espousing. Let's review two examples that touch on many of the most common platforms for delivery, beginning in the arena of sales.

Vodafone Academy WAP Performance Modules

A recent project with Vodafone called for ten Web-based training modules. Since Vodafone is the largest cellular network in the world, it made sense it would also request that some portion of the content be deliverable over a WAP phone. Knowing that we would be asked to produce the subset of the entire course in a wireless format, let us begin planning from the audience analysis phase all the way through to implementation.

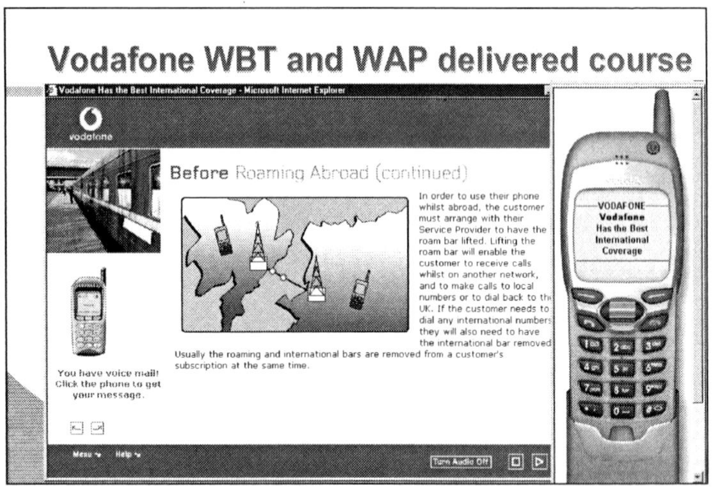

For the analysis phase, we were able to project the target audience along with several sample use scenarios, and pilot these with both the client and several representative users to see if our assumptions were correct. The analysis also allowed us to think through some of the technical considerations facing deployment on various networks with assorted phone handsets and WAP devices.

We were also able to determine that, in most cases, the audience would be looking to the WAP content as a reminder or memory aid rather than a first exposure. The WAP content would also need to serve as a teaser to encourage people to go to the Web and take the full online course. The memory aid model would be useful for sales representatives who need quick access to the features and benefits of the Vodafone network. A multiple-level strategy would allow the learner to drill deeper into the explanation of each benefit, but the information would not nearly be to the depth of the Web content found in the courses.

After we planned the work and completed our analysis, it was time to design the WAP content. The hardest part of this process is the information design—in relationship to the structure of content—for a small screen and limited bandwidth ill-suited for large graphics or long blocks of text. It takes longer than one might expect to define levels of information and a framework taxonomy for a large information space.

One design principle that proves quite useful is the inverted pyramid model of writing found in newspaper journalism. In this model, the designer or writer provides a summary with all pertinent information, and then goes into more detail in the paragraphs that follow. These paragraphs can be structured as hyperlinks within the context of a WAP browser.

Care should be taken to provide an appropriate number of choices for each page. On the Web, 7+/-2 is used as a benchmark because of the typical cognitive ability limitations of remembering discrete pockets of information. On the handheld device or phone handset, this number should be reduced to 4+/-2. This is based on the logistics of a small screen, number of display lines, and the distinct possibility of the learner processing other information such as feedback from the handset as she presses buttons to scroll through the interface.

Some of the distinctions of the learners' usage patterns can be discovered during the development of preliminary WAP content templates, which allow you to pour content into a fixed, standard structure for navigating through the information. Once the information structure is designed, you can begin populating it with learning content.

During the development phase, the key factors are writing style and following through on the content structure detailed during the design phase. For example, it is necessary to write or edit the content for delivery on a small screen. As a development practice, we asked our writers to limit their content for a single screen to the amount they could write on one-fourth of a 3” × 5” note card. This limitation helped focus the wordsmithing and made the final format apparent throughout the development process.

Since then, we have started using a database with a defined field length as a limiter. It is not enough to simply cut down the amount of text; the breaks in information must be logical and as close to lines of Reusable Learning Objects (RLOs) or Reusable Information Objects (RIOs) as possible. Following a Learning Objects model will also help you reuse some of the same content, but in a different form. After the learning content is developed and placed within the taxonomy, you are ready to put the content into the WAP information framework from the design phase.

The implementation phase includes placing the content into the technical framework, which in this case is WAP’s WML (Wireless Markup Language). An automated process for pouring the content into the infrastructure can greatly decrease the time involved, but often proves impractical for smaller amounts of content or complex linking of content.

Testing is another important part of the implementation process. It is very important to post the content to a Web server that can deliver WAP content and access it from a variety of different browsers. Concerning Web content delivered to browsers such as Netscape Navigator and Microsoft Internet Explorer, it is very likely you will encounter anomalies related to certain phones or WAP browsers. In part, this is due to the relative newness of the technology and the variance in WAP browser types.

After you have thoroughly tested your learning content internally, the real test takes place: rolling out the training to your intended audience. As you gather anecdotal feedback from users, it is important to evaluate these results in relationship to the overall learning program, including training in other formats and from other sources.

Evaluating wireless eLearning is more difficult than other types of learning because of the instant, rapid learning process involved when it is done correctly. Imagine asking a learner to fill out a sheet documenting every time they smile, or take a short test after every instant of looking up key information while on the job. The instrument would interfere with the results because of the time demand and the annoyance of having to give input on a device known for its poorer input capabilities.

One way to perform ongoing evaluations in a more structured fashion is through survey instruments delivered on the Web or via e-mail. Some organizations also conduct focus group studies to examine the usability patterns and record fixes or augmentations based on both the learning content effectiveness, and the technical and interface suitability of the solution.

3Com® University Uses the Palm™ for Mobile eLearning

The business of 3Com University depends on reaching internal and external sales consultants, technicians, and customers with timely information about the features, benefits, and technical specifications of its products. As an innovator in the field of personal digital assistants (PDAs), 3Com was perfectly positioned to undertake a pilot project to demonstrate the usefulness of offering instant information about 3Com products to customers, consultants, and technicians who were working in the field using a Palm handheld device.

The Strategy

RWD Technologies® worked with 3Com to identify a strategy enabling the Palm to deliver just-in-time information to a mobile and geographically diverse target population. Once the technical and design strategy was in place, 3Com's HomeConnect and OfficeConnect products were selected to form the initial knowledge base. RWD then developed and built two modules that contain product features, benefits and technical specifications, as well as a self-assessment where users can check their HomeConnect and OfficeConnect product knowledge.

Currently, anyone can download data modules from the 3Com University Web site to the Palm and get the latest product information. The modules can be used with any Palm. "Being able to deliver education via the Palm, specifically in a downloadable format, has given us a unique avenue to provide information to our students," says Robert Jackson, 3Com IT Project Manager. "They can realize the benefits of the Palm with instant-on, extreme portability, and easy access to information, all without having to take 10 minutes to boot up their 12-pound laptops. It truly is training at your fingertips."

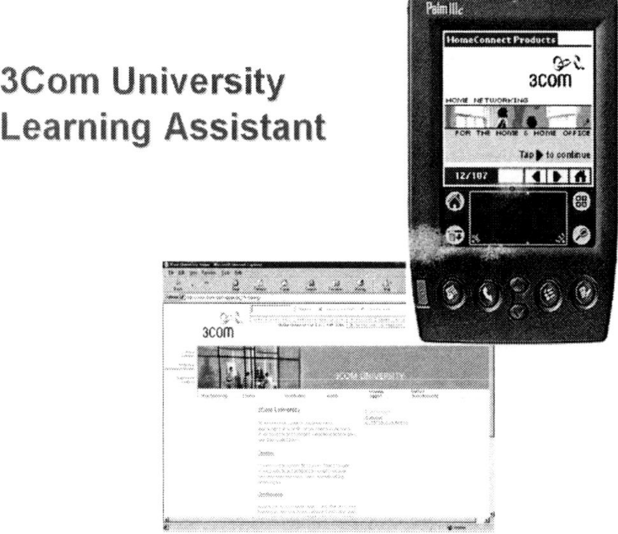

The inclusion of performance-oriented solutions such as the Palm-based mLearning, combined with access to a knowledge management system, Enterprise Tools, a learning management and online testing system, allows for a blended eLearning solution for 3Com University.

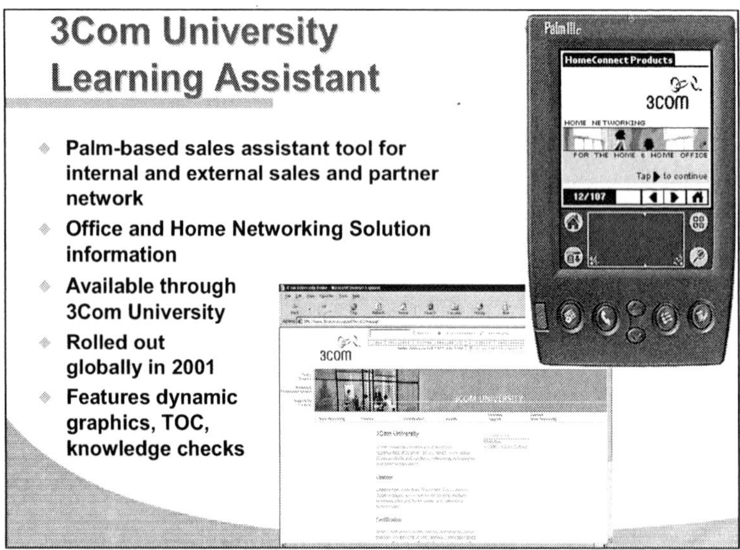

The Features

The 3Com University Learning Assistant includes important features such as easy-to-use navigation, bookmarks to save your last place in a module, and a favorites list. It also includes knowledge checks (a basic multiple-choice self-assessment), advanced graphics capabilities for color and grayscale graphics, and easy-to-update and synchronize data modules. Finding an easy-to-use tool that met the technical and design requirements was not an easy task, but a firm understanding of the development options helped make the decision process easier. In addition, new products are continuously emerging and providing added functionality.

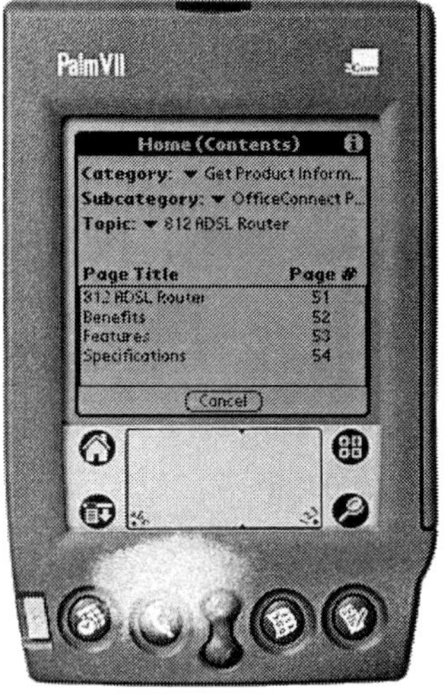

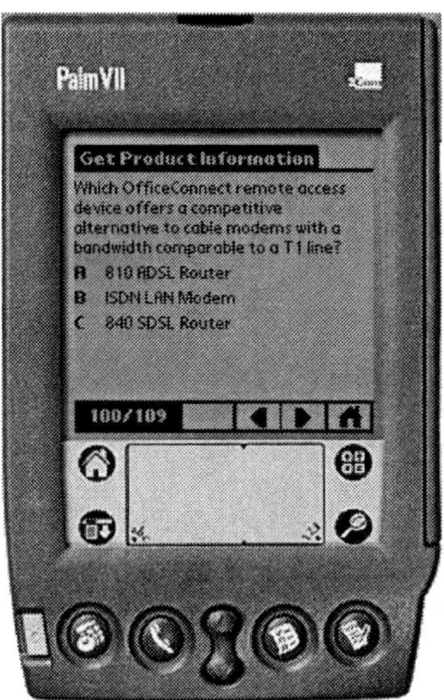

The Solution

This solution enables 3Com University to take a lead in providing learning materials for delivery to mobile devices (see quote below). The Palm delivery strategy also makes it easier for people to have up-to-date information with them at all times. The Learning Assistant is easy to use; beyond the instant availability of information, the module knowledge checks reinforce actual learning.

> "Being able to deliver education via the Palm, specifically in a downloadable format, has given us a unique avenue to provide information to our students."
>
> *Robert Jackson, 3Com IT Project Manager*

"We expect the Learning Assistant will become a valuable tool in the hands of our sales teams around the globe," adds Geoff Roberts, director of 3Com University.

Let us now turn our focus to some examples of how mLearning can create greater efficiency and, hence, greater productivity in the area of professional services.

Conclusion

Can you use mLearning in your sales organization? Many other companies are rolling out systems that link to CRM (Customer Relationship Management) Systems, which we'll examine further in Chapter Nine. Next we'll review cases that link mobile to learning for services roles.

Chapter Five:
Case Studies—Services

The busy person in the field servicing clients needs to maximize his or her minutes and fully address as many customer needs as possible within a given work day. The three examples that follow show how mLearning can allow for faster and more complete productivity in the hands of those who stand in the gap between the company and the client.

Wireless e-Learning IP Troubleshooting Field Guide for the Palm VII

This author played an integral role with RWD Technologies in the first award-winning mobile learning project that won the Gold Award for Innovation in the Brandon-Hall of Fame Awards for 2000. The following is an overview of the IP Troubleshooting Field Guide application and some discussion about the constructivist learning model used to produce this performance-based training module.

Overview

As we built this early wireless e-learning application for the Palm VII, we had to reevaluate our thinking on learning models and technical capabilities that work on a small screen with minimal bandwidth capabilities. Putting ourselves in the position of the end-user—field service technician out on a client call—really helped us solidify the approach we took.

The initial goal was to provide a very thin front-end interface to a vast repository of step-by-step tutorials on some of the most common TCP/IP configuration problems. This information can be accessed from anywhere, anytime. As stated in previous chapters, we call this just-in-time, just-in-place learning.

Combining Performance Support

Once we built the tutorials and did some initial focus studies, it felt like something was missing. For the field technician, we realized that the first step might in fact be the need to request new hardware. Sometimes there is no way to salvage damaged or defective equipment.

This need gave birth to the Field Replacement Unit (FRU) request that links back to a home office database. While we realized that this is more aptly described as performance support, we felt it was an important step. Also, much of the work that we did at RWD was based on Hybrid eLearning and Performance Support solutions.

Learning Approach

When looking at the step-by-step tutorials, many people have asked the question, "...but is it training?" The answer is yes. Technicians learn how to do new things and also have access to information that is vast and hard to memorize. In complex knowledge domains where people have an intermediate to advanced level of skill, a constructivist learning approach is sometimes more appropriate instead of the more common objectivist approach.

Constructivism allows the learner to create their own learning paths to the information they need within a structured body of knowledge. This learning model is also uniquely appropriate to designing learning applications for handheld devices.

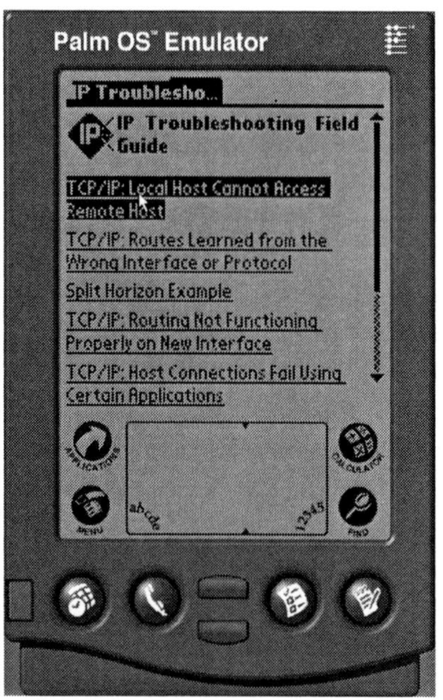

Reworking Content

Because of the small size and bandwidth, we also ran into issues with writing style and screen format. Long narrative is less effective than short steps and sequenced commands. The interface for the learner/technician is designed to give them the right information, at the right time, in the fewest number of clicks, and with the minimum amount of extraneous information. Screen size and color depth (white, black, and two grays) also was an issue that we had to work around. Large diagrams had to be broken down into smaller, linked units. Some had to be turned sideways so that they could be scrolled across.

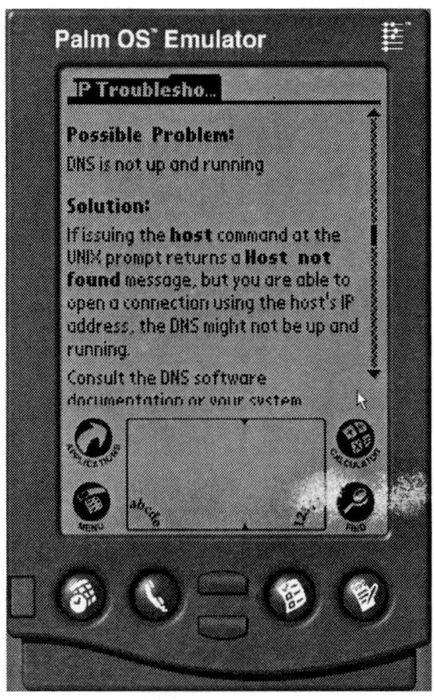
Palm OS Emulator
IP Troublesho...
Possible Problem:
DNS is not up and running
Solution:
If issuing the host command at the UNIX prompt returns a Host not found message, but you are able to open a connection using the host's IP address, the DNS might not be up and running.
Consult the DNS software

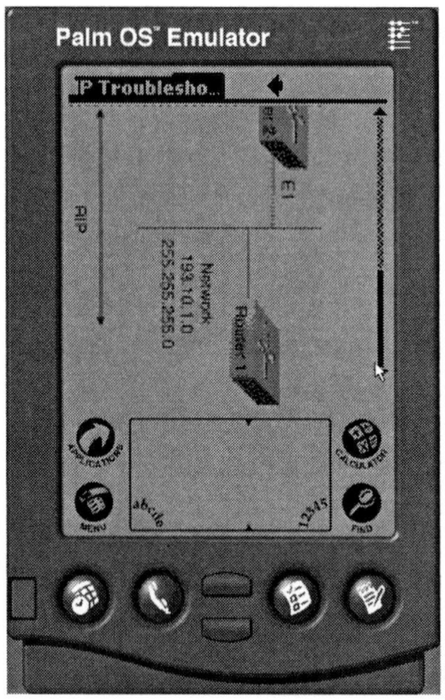

Next Steps

This demonstration is a first step. In the process, we have identified many new capabilities and functions that would be useful to include. For instance, a search link could be used to search for information about specific error codes across the entire domain of information. This more detailed search may be useful for highly skilled technicians who do not want the descriptions of the symptoms and problems, just short performance aids so that they do not have to remember every command and step for operations that are performed infrequently.

Smart Phones

RWD also repurposed part of the module for delivery over Internet-enabled smart phones and other wireless devices for greater accessibility beyond the Palm network. For global deployment, using these Wireless Application Protocol (WAP) enabled phones is preferable.

Valero's Mobile Procedure Access

Another example of extending the reach of the typical mobile employee and the typical office worker involves quality inspections that are done in field locations.

The company example that we are using here is from Valero Energy for a pilot study conducted several years ago with handheld (and practically handtop) devices. These devices had the full Windows 95 or Windows 98 operating systems on them, and had a touch-screen interface that made it easy to have all of the documentation one would need for quality inspections along with forms that can be filled out using a handheld, slate-oriented device.

Some of the areas of exploration for next generation activity around these quality inspections center on the use of even smaller devices like PDAs. Several test studies were done, similar to the one listed here, that use some of the exact documentation from Adobe Acrobat that was used on the handtop Internet device delivered out to the even smaller PDA devices like the palm shown on the next page.

A key feature is the ability to access these complex diagrams and to have word documents that serve as both work instructions and PDF viewer documents, easily accessible in either black or white.

Is this learning you might ask? Again we are looking at a model that centers on people's workplace performance and learning within a context of a particular work flow of quality inspections. Understanding this audience and context shows that performance support is the right performance intervention and solution to be able to deliver the information right when someone needs it, when they are away from their desk and computer, and might need access to something in the field when they are inspecting a particular system.

This is an important component of the overall solution that drives getting the right information in the right hands, at the right time, for the right people. Understanding how this affects the outcomes of work from the standpoint of quality and time off task, before someone can get back to their actual work, is an important part of understanding how mLearning can be integrated into the core work flow of daily activities.

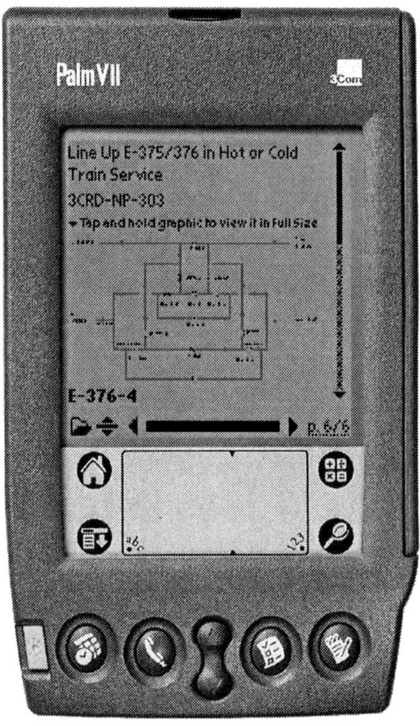

Real-Time and Work Flow–Based Learning in the U.S. Defense Industry

By Harvey Singh

The brief scenario below highlights work flow–based learning in action, based on a project for the U.S. Navy. The project represents a sophisticated form of blended learning in which learning, performance support, and job task–based workspace environment are all integrated together to deliver context-based knowledge to support and augment job tasks at hand.

Field customer service technicians in the military work in a challenging and knowledge-intensive environment in which they need to support multiple requests or customer problems, including maintenance, repair, part replacement, installation of complex equipment, and so forth. In order to perform these complex tasks, field service technicians need on-demand access to procedures, manuals, schematics, learning, and technical data.

While these technicians are trained and go through certifications, they need access to complex sets of information in a highly mobile and fast-paced work environment. Long sequences of eLearning courses do not provide an adequate model to support day-to-day field technician knowledge needs.

Real-time work flow–based learning is embedded in the field technician's workspace portal in which the tasks are assigned and presented, along with the package of documents, performance objects (procedures and step-by-step instructions), and other reference information required to perform the tasks (see Figure 1—illustrated with an analogous case from the telecom industry since Department of Defense materials could not be used).

The field technician can download the task information along with supporting materials onto a mobile device so that the information can be pulled up during the performance of the tasks (see Figure 2). The technician can pass on queries or information from the field and forward it on to the corporate office through an automated work flow process. The technician can also connect with other peers or experts via conferencing to get "live" mentoring to help perform a non-routine task. Field technicians can also access eLearning modules, technical manuals, and parts/technical data in a Web and mobile environment.

Figure 1
Work Flow Learning Portal for Field Service Technicians

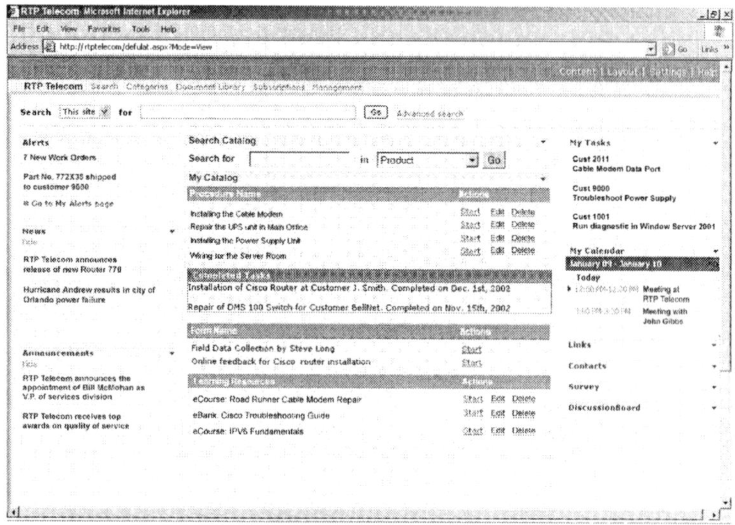

Source: Harvey Singh

The task and work flow status is tracked in real time, along with the time and path taken to perform the tasks. Aggregated data is presented using management dashboards/portals for performance analysis, rapid decisions, and remediation (to correct in bottlenecks, prioritize task, plan resources and skills, and manage training needs).

Figure 2
Portable Devices Used by Field Service Technicians

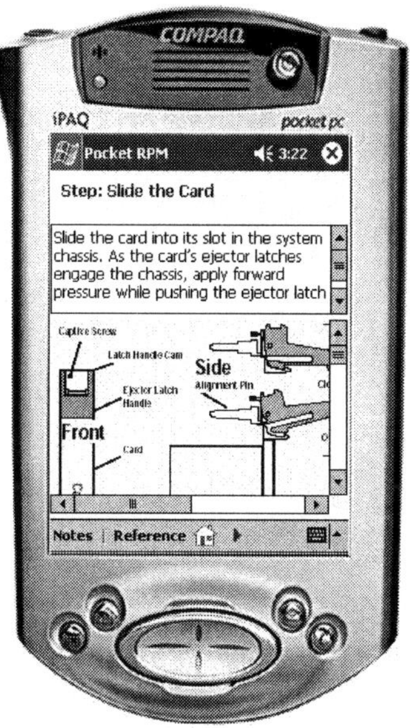

Source: Instancy, Inc.

In Chapter Ten, we will explore in depth another example involving work for SimplexGrinnell in Tyco's Fire and Security Division, which provides fire suppression systems—such as sprinkler heads—for buildings across the world. In the meantime, we now proceed to our final chapter of focused case studies, with a spotlight on mLearning opportunities for the strategic marketing teams of corporations.

Chapter Six:
Case Studies—Business Processes and Performance

Introduction

Finally, in this concluding chapter of case studies, we will examine how companies have integrated mLearning techniques into their processes of doing business and enhancing performance. The details that follow may take some time to absorb, but they tell a compelling story of how the face of business is rapidly changing in light of emerging technologies.

ALLTEL

By Kate Franks
Contributed by Matthew Nehrling

Need/Opportunity

In July 2004, ALLTEL's wireless data revenue was only $6 million per month, significantly less than the industry average. The company sought to improve this figure and capitalize on the fact that Super Bowl XXXIX would be held at ALLTEL Stadium in Jacksonville, Florida.

In February 2005, ALLTEL's marketing department created a consumer sweepstakes in which customers registered to win one of five trips to the Super Bowl and $1 million each time they sent a text or picture message or downloaded a ring tone or game application. The challenge presented to the company's corporate communications department was to create an employee campaign to engage employees in text messaging and involve them in the largest consumer campaign in the company's history. The campaign was also needed to boost employee morale.

Consumers were given free text messaging for the month of September. Employees were offered a free text-messaging package of 300 outgoing and unlimited incoming messages for the term of their employment with ALLTEL. The campaign started in mid-August with communication about signing up for the employee text-messaging rate plan and continued through the fourth quarter.

Intended Audience

The target audience was ALLTEL's 13,500 employees in 26 states, including:

- 2,500 employees at corporate headquarters in Little Rock, Arkansas
- 6,000 retail employees in 500 locations
- 5,000 call center employees at 14 locations around the country

The campaign was designed to encourage text messaging on ALLTEL's network, but employees outside ALLTEL wireless properties were invited to participate using another wireless carrier or via e-mail.

Goals and Objectives

The employee campaign had the following objectives:

1. Engage employees in ALLTEL's consumer campaign goal of increasing wireless data revenue to $20 million per month by December 31, 2004. (The financial forecast for 2004 was $14 million.)
2. Make wireless data services part of ALLTEL's culture.
3. Integrate the consumer "Txt2Win MVP Sweepstakes" promotion with employee activities.

Solution Overview

ALLTEL employees had the opportunity to participate in an employee version of the Txt2Win MVP Sweepstakes. Employees across the country were eligible to win $10,000, one of three trips for two to Super Bowl XXXIX at ALLTEL Stadium, or weekly prizes. The promotion was divided into four primary campaigns:

1. All employees were eligible to compete in a 17-week text-message–based trivia contest. NFL- and ALLTEL-related trivia questions were delivered via text message every Friday, and employees had until 5:00 p.m. the following Monday to reply.
2. A drawing for Super Bowl prize #1 was held for all sales employees who met monthly quotas for each of the four months of the campaign.

3. Employees at the Little Rock campus were divided by floor into 32 NFL teams to compete for Super Bowl prize #2. The Super Bowl Prize #2 drawing was held at the end of the regular NFL season for all participants on the team with the most victories. Each floor competed in weekly match-ups based on the actual NFL schedule, and the winners of each week's games were determined by the percent of correct answers to the weekly trivia questions. Those individuals who answered the most questions correctly were eligible for the $10,000 grand prize. The 32 NFL coaches and their assistants served as a valuable communication tool throughout the campaign. We sent messages to the coaches, and they forwarded them to each of their team members.
4. All employees outside Little Rock were eligible to compete for Super Bowl prize #3. They registered to receive a single trivia question via text message on Friday, January 7. A drawing was held for everyone who answered the question correctly by 5:00 p.m. the following Monday.

Additional contests were held throughout the four-month campaign to illustrate different ways text messaging can be used and to keep momentum for the campaign high throughout the 17-week NFL season:

- **Coaches' Meeting – Kick off Event (August 26)**
  Coaches were recruited and briefed about the Txt2Win contest. Teams were assigned by allowing all 32 coaches to simultaneously throw a football with their name on it into one of 32 team boxes in the front of the auditorium. Each coach received the team box with his or her football inside. The team boxes included an official NFL jersey, baseball cap and mini helmet, written instructions for the Txt2Win MVP campaign for each member of the team, team schedules, a $50 gift card for floor decorations, a clipboard and team roster, a whistle, and a bottle of Gatorade.

- **Pep Rally (September 10)**
  Executive Management led all 32 teams in a festive pep rally to kick off the employee campaign. More than 1,500 employees gathered along the Arkansas River behind corporate headquarters and watched as the CEO shot t-shirts into the crowd with an air gun. Other executives donned black and red scarves on their heads and carried swords in support of their assigned team, the Tampa Bay Buccaneers. The jumbo-tron broadcast of the event featured trivia questions that employees responded to via text message. More than 200 answers were submitted for each of the four questions. Winners received tickets to upcoming Arkansas Razorbacks games and season tickets to the Arkansas Twisters, an AF2 team that plays at ALLTEL Arena. Twisters' Coach Gary Anderson led the crowd in thumb exercises to start the event. A spirit contest roll call of teams followed. A noise meter was featured on the

jumbo-tron with each team's results. The winning team received a free lunch, and members of four Spirit Award finalist teams had an opportunity to submit an entry for one of five individual prizes.

- **Rescue Frank! (September 22)**
  As employees arrived on the Little Rock campus, they were welcomed with loud music and Executive Vice President-Marketing Frank O'Mara trapped on the roof of the Building 5 driveway canopy. Employees in Little Rock were asked to refrain from talking on their wireless phone until O'Mara reached his goal of 1,000 text messages.

- **Floor Decorating Contest (September 23)**
  Each team received a $50 gift card to decorate their floor with their NFL team colors. Three local celebrities, including a local sports anchor and two professional decorators, one of whom decorated the White House during President Bill Clinton's term, served as judges. They were escorted throughout the campus to view each floor. The winning team, the Dallas Cowboys, greeted the judges with a swarm of photographers and videographers. A Dallas Cowboys cheerleader gave the judges a tour of the team's offices after a brief meeting with the head coach. Enthusiastic fans greeted the judges along the way chanting "We're No.1, You're No. 2. We're going to beat the Txt out of you!" The tour ended at the team's locker room, which was filled with steam. Judges were presented with VIP credentials, cookies with the team logo, customized bottles of water, and personalized towels with a Dallas

Cowboys VIP logo. The Atlanta Falcons transformed their floor into the Georgia Dome with a mural of fan faces around the entire floor. The Rams' floor featured a locker room complete with weight machines, lockers, and showers. When the judges arrived, four employees rolled up their pants and hid behind the shower curtain as a bubble machine blew bubbles into the air.

- **Ryan Newman Day (November 2)**
  NASCAR star Ryan Newman, driver of the No. 12 ALLTEL Dodge, visited the corporate office to sign autographs and meet employees. Employees had an opportunity to meet Ryan and win autographed merchandise by sending in a message with the time closest to the time of his fastest pit stop in an upcoming race.

- **Goodwill Bonus Wins (November 12 and December 8)**
  Little Rock–based teams had a chance to earn bonus wins by participating in two separate charity events on the ALLTEL campus for the American Red Cross Blood Drive and Arkansas Foodbank Network Food Drive. Teams could also compete to win lunch for their team by collecting used wireless phones for ALLTEL's enhanced recycling program.

- **Christmas Tree Decorating Contest (December 13–17)**
  Each coach received a pre-lit, 4-foot Christmas tree and a $50 allowance for decorations. The decorated trees were placed in three common areas of the Little Rock campus, and employees

voted by text message for their favorite tree. We also held a silent auction of the trees benefiting the ALLTEL Charitable Fund, a fund to help employees who have suffered a medical emergency or loss due to fire, flood, tornado, or other disasters.

- **Candy Cane Contest (December 22–January 7)** Each Little Rock team member received a candy cane tagged with instructions and a unique number. By text messaging the number on their candy cane tag to a designated phone number, they found out if they were one of 100 winners of a $20 gift card.
- **Prize Winner Announcement (January 12)** Eligible employees were invited to the announcement of the $10,000 and Super Bowl Packages winners. Those outside of Little Rock joined the festivities via conference call. CEO Scott Ford and local sportscaster Craig O'Neill announced the winners by calling the winning cell phone numbers on a speakerphone. In addition to two Super Bowl prize winners and the $10,000 winner, 39 employees won $100 prizes in honor of Super Bowl XXXIX at ALLTEL Stadium.

Communication Tools

Internal communication tools included the 32 Little Rock coaches along with more traditional vehicles. ALLTEL's Intranet, ALLTEL Today, was used throughout the campaign. Txt2Win was a permanent link on the Intranet and served as an archive of ALLTEL Today stories and videos on the contest, rules and FAQ's, recap of the trivia questions and standings, photos, and other related links to the campaign (i.e., Super Bowl Web site). Mass e-mails were also sent company-wide throughout the campaign. Text messaging was used to lead employees to the Intranet for important announcements about the campaign and other company news.

Sales Campaign

The sales channel employees who met or exceeded all wireless and feature quotas were entered in a drawing to win Super Bowl trips. To kick off the campaign, each of ALLTEL's 600 call center and retail locations received a "Tailgate-in-a-Box." Each box included Txt2Win megaphones, footballs, popcorn, magnets, shirts, pens, confetti, buttons, and pom poms for each employee.

Implementation and Challenges

Before launching the internal campaign, senior management provided feedback on the initial pitch for this campaign. Focus groups were conducted with presidents of retail services, wireless presidents, area managers, and wireline presidents. From meetings with these key areas of the company, feedback included the following:

- The sales contest changed to be based on cumulative sales. If a sales person did not meet quota during the first month, they remained eligible for prizes.
- An e-mail feature was added for employees in ALLTEL wireline properties without ALLTEL wireless service and for employees who use another

> wireless carrier. For those areas that were strictly wireline, e-mails were sent to the area administrator to post the trivia questions, and answers were sent via e-mail to the corporate communications department. Those areas participating in the e-mail campaign were sent a "Tailgate-in-a-Box" as well.

Total budget for the campaign was $200,000. Actual expenses were approximately $190,512. A cost breakdown is provided on the next page.

Campaign Budget

Cash Grand Prize	$ 10,000	Team Lunch Prizes	$ 2,000	Weekly Prizes	$ 2,000
3 Super Bowl Trips	18,000	Sales Contest	65,000	Staging	12,000
Promotional Merchandise	70,000	Christmas Tree Contest	4,000	Printing	312
Coaches' Materials	5,000	Candy Cane Promotion	2,200	Advertising	0

The external campaign was tied to Super Bowl XXXIX. Since ALLTEL was not an official Super Bowl sponsor, there were licensing challenges in developing campaign materials and obtaining all the required approvals. ALLTEL secured pass-through rights with the NFL and Super Bowl XXXIX with Motorola, a long-term vendor of wireless phones for ALLTEL. Terms of this agreement prevented the consumer campaign from advertising rate plans or products other than the Motorola phones ALLTEL sells, thus limiting the campaign's placement in the fourth quarter promotions mix. Because of these limitations, grassroots efforts by employees to promote the consumer campaign were vital for its success, thus making it necessary to engage all employees in the campaign.

Measurement/Evaluation of Outcomes

The results of the campaign demonstrate that ALLTEL's employee Txt2Win MVP Sweepstakes met and exceeded its objectives.

1. Engage employees in ALLTEL's goal of increasing data revenue to $20 million/month. (The financial forecast for 2004 was $14 million.)

    - Wireless data service billings for November reached $13.3 million, up 42 percent from October.
    - Wireless data billings for December topped $15 million, exceeding the year-end forecast of $14 million.
    - Employees sent and received more than 325,000 messages as part of the employee campaign.

- Sales of text messaging packages (i.e., 50 incoming and 50 outgoing text messages for $2.99) increased 61 percent during the campaign. Annual incremental revenue from the increase of text messaging packages in the fourth quarter is $10.5 million.
- Revenue from text messaging increased 59 percent in the fourth quarter.

2. Make wireless data services part of ALLTEL's culture.

- More than 92 percent of 2,500 Little Rock employees at five office locations registered to participate on their assigned team.
- More than 6,000 employees (44 percent) outside Little Rock registered their text message–enabled phone for the contest.
- Employees used text messaging weekly to submit answers for the trivia contest.
- Text messaging reminders were used throughout the campaign.
- Separate databases of wireless phone numbers for the 2,500 corporate headquarters employees and those outside Little Rock were developed, realizing that we'd have different messages for these audiences.
- A database of wireless phone numbers for employees was created and could be used as a means to quickly communicate with employees. Text messaging now serves as a valuable communication tool to relay information such as snow

days, blood drives, and other special events for Little Rock employees.

- For the Rescue Frank! event, 10,044 text messages were sent in three hours.
- Ryan Newman received 1,159 text messages during Ryan Newman Day.
- 540 employees answered all weekly questions correctly and were eligible to win the $10,000.
- More than 320 employees dialed in to participate in the January 12 announcement conference call. Another 300 employees attended the event on the Little Rock campus.

3. Integrate customer "Txt2Win MVP Sweepstakes" promotion with employee activities.

    - Both the employee and consumer campaigns required participants to use text messaging from their wireless phones.
    - Like the consumer campaign, employees had a chance to win a cash prize, Super Bowl trips, and weekly prizes.
    - The employee trivia questions featured NFL football and ALLTEL.
    - Employees helped with grassroots efforts to encourage consumers to participate in the consumer campaign. 100,000 copies of the instructions were printed on business-card–sized paper and given to all employees for distribution.

- Text messaging and the Txt2Win campaign were integrated into traditional holiday activities:
  - Little Rock employees collected 4,308 pounds of food to benefit the Arkansas Food Bank Network. Each team received a win for donating at least 150 items.
  - More than 1,000 no-longer-used wireless phones were donated in support of ALLTEL's enhanced recycling program.
  - Nearly 200 employees helped set a record for participation at the American Red Cross blood drive at ALLTEL's corporate headquarters in Little Rock on December 8. Employees donated more than 167 productive units, passing both the drive goal of 150 units and the previous record of 130 units. Each team received a win if six team members donated blood.
  - Through the Txt2Win Christmas tree decorating and silent auction, employees raised $1,118.50 for the ALLTEL Charitable Fund, and 486 text messages were sent from employees to vote on the best-decorated tree.

QUALCOMM, Inc.

By Clark Quinn,
Director of User Experience, Knowledge Anywhere

QUALCOMM, Inc. is the force behind two major technologies: Code Division Multiple Access (CDMA), an international wireless standard, and Binary Run time Environment for Wireless (BREW), a cross-platform mobile application development environment.

As a standard-bearer for mobile applications, the company wanted to develop an mLearning implementation. An existing instructor-led course on the subject of negotiation was chosen as the source material. An explicit decision was made not to reproduce the course in its entirety online, but instead to develop augmenting materials. Knowledge Anywhere, an experienced eLearning solutions provider with previous mobile and performance support experience, was chosen to develop the mobile learning adjunct.

The target audience for the mobile learning product was QUALCOMM employees taking the course in negotiation, though a broader market opportunity was always a consideration. Negotiation is a difficult and important skill for individuals. Steve Wilders of the Jackson Wilders Group developed a theoretically strong and practically effective course, which was both the central element around which the adjunct was developed and the final source of the content.

The target devices for the content were two LG phones, the VX 4400 and the VX 6000. These two phones share a 15 character wide screen, with either a seven- or eight-line usable screen area. It was an underlying premise of the project that mobile learning is not *eLearning Lite*™, and consequently, an online course squeezed onto such a

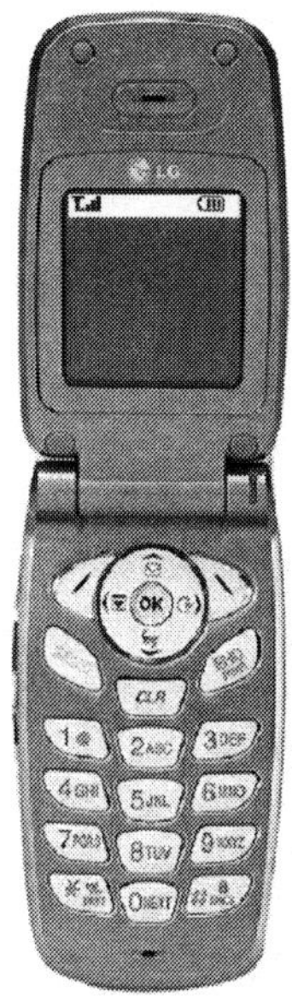

LG VX 4400 and VX 6000

screen factor would not make sense. The goal had to be a way to reinforce and augment the instructor-led course in ways that made sense for the target devices.

Wilders developed some initial concepts for mobile adjuncts to the course, which were brought into a joint effort toward identifying an effective approach. The challenge was to think of potential augmenting activities.

One of the benefits of mobile devices is the ability to make small bits of knowledge available during moments when we are not otherwise occupied. Much of formal learning is focused on an "event" model, where the learner leaves the performance context and spends time acquiring new skills.

This knowledge can atrophy rapidly post-event. The possibility of having a mobile device possessing the capability of reactivating the relevant knowledge provides new support for effective learning.

We know that several activities help reinforce learning, including drilling necessary background knowledge to ensure it is sufficiently automatic for use at the point and time of need, and practice on using that knowledge in relevant contexts. Consequently, two major components of the mobile learning adjunct were a series of multiple-choice questions that drilled important knowledge, and a series of scenarios that allowed learners to explore the application of that knowledge to particular situations.

One of the realities of the workplace, however, is the necessity to use knowledge before it has been acquired or perfected. As a consequence, a performance support system strategy was developed to scaffold individuals in action before they acquired the necessary complete suite of skills. A third component was also proposed that supported the task of preparing for and conducting a negotiation.

With the three-pronged approach of knowledge test, scenario practice, and performance support confirmed, the initial information architecture was undertaken. An initial design had a top-level menu of the three choices that included:

- A Quiz component with a series of questions to be presented (with feedback upon answers) for the knowledge test;
- A Scenarios component with a series of scenarios offering options for actions and consequences (with feedback) for each choice; and

- A Performance Support System with two components, a section of 10 Reminders tailored to the most important components and a Planning Tool section structured around the major components of the negotiation process that drilled down to sub-steps and provided specific questions to be answered during the process.

A diagram of the proposed approach is shown on the following page.

Qualcomm Three-Pronged Approach

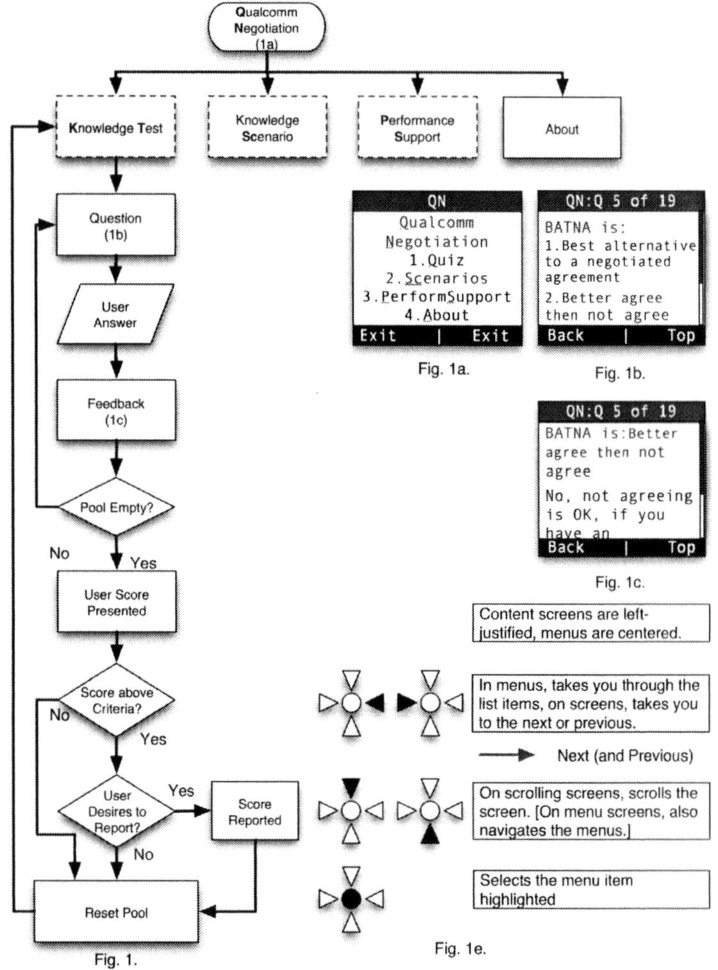

Fig. 1. Fig. 1a. Fig. 1b. Fig. 1c. Fig. 1e.

Information Architecture for the Review (with Storyboard of Screens and Jog-Dial Navigation)

Steve Wilders had developed rich initial text-based content, but the limited screen real estate posed significant problems. After several content "digestion" steps, there were still problems containing the relevant information to one screen of content. As a consequence, two obvious strategies were used: information that could be chunked was spread across multiple screens, and scrolling was tolerated when critical content extended past the screen limit.

The graphics below illustrate how various forms of content were displayed:

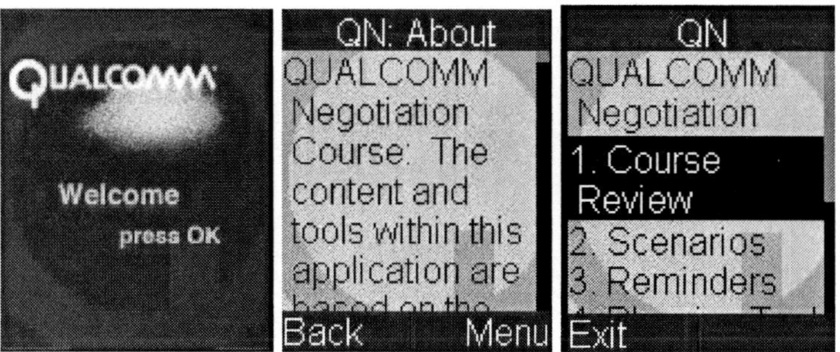

Splash Screen, About, and Top Menu

A number of interface decisions also had to be made. While the availability of several buttons, and the traditional jog-dial interface (left, right, up, down, and a select button) were available, it was non-trivial to map all the desired navigation and specification tasks to these buttons. Several iterations of approaches were taken. Details were reviewed, refined, and tested.

The graphics below illustrate use of headers as well as Back and Menu button directives.

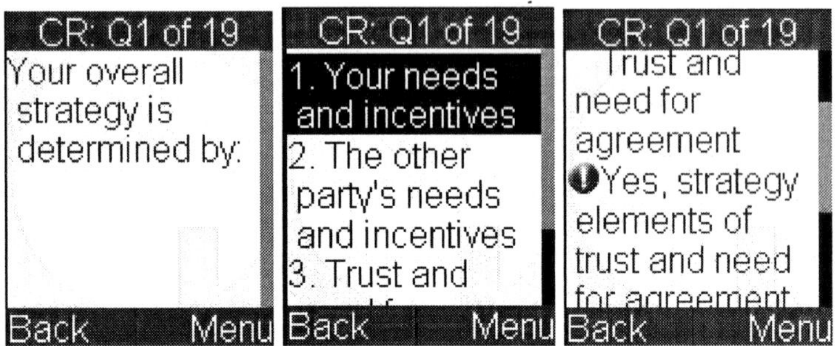

Review Question, Response Options, and Feedback

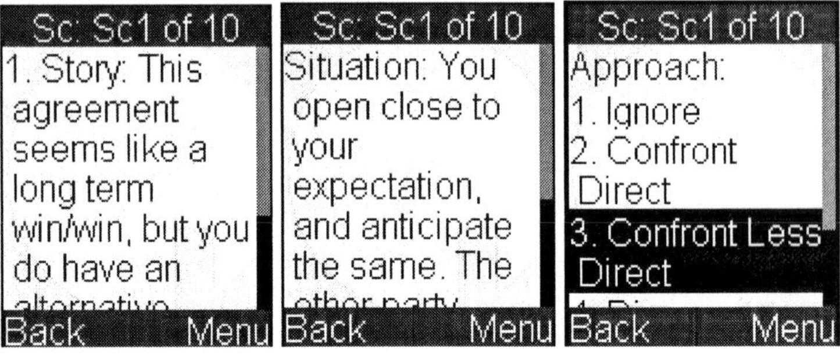

Scenario Story, Situation, Response Options, and Outcome

Other factors influenced the resulting system. For instance, the initial architecture with three components eventually was broken up into four. The Performance Support choice was removed and the two subcomponents, "Reminders" and "Planning Tool," became their own top-level options. This traded off conceptual coherence for simplified navigation.

The graphics below illustrate these two components.

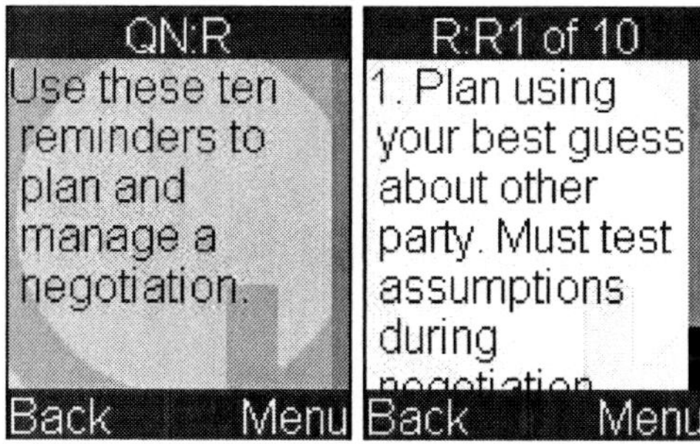

Ten Reminders Start and Example

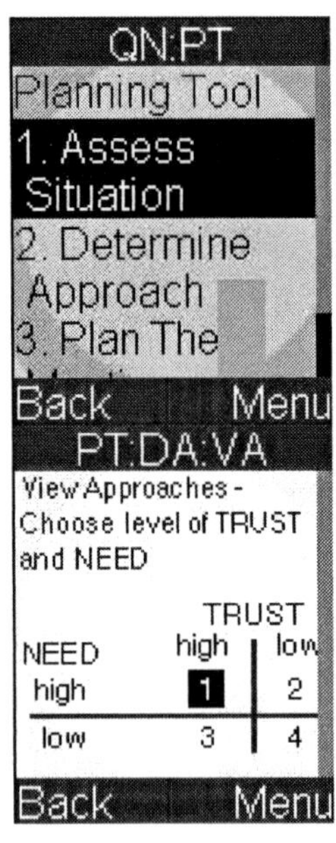

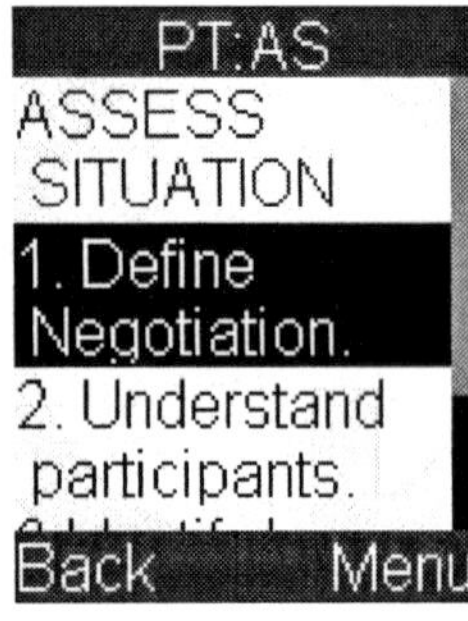

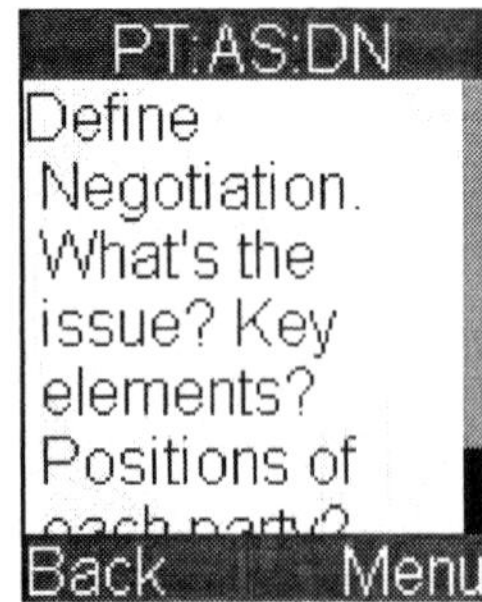

Planning Top Level,
Next Level, Questions to Ask,
and Assessment Matrix

Knowledge test scores and data about the use of the Scenarios, Reminders, and Planning Tool components are databased on a server. A subset of this data is uploaded to a Learning Management System (LMS) for tracking purposes.

The resulting implementation is being prepared for release as this text is being composed. Deployment will begin with QUALCOMM employees.

Nokia Quality WAP Modules for Methods and Tools

Nokia's internal quality group began developing Web-based training modules for internal methods and tools that ensure its high quality products. Web-based modules were built using HTML and Flash technology for deployment in their internal LCMS. The modules conform to SCORM learning standards and have been deployed globally.

In addition to the core WBT modules, several other innovative approaches to learning were deployed. One was the use of discussion boards to promote cooperative learning and construction or sharing of new ideas. The other was a performance-driven approach to delivering

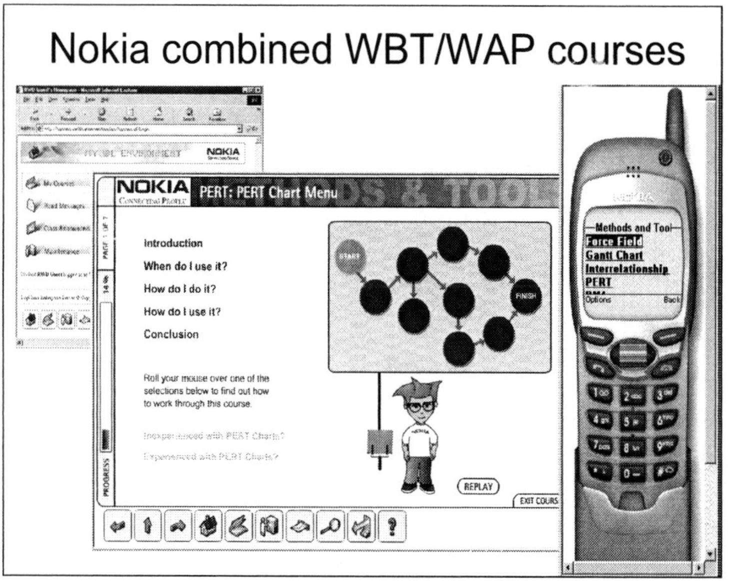

WAP-based modules that were, in essence, a condensed version of the course content. A structured format describing each tool (such as Pert charting), what it looks like, how to use it, and specific Nokia procedures were provided. The two methods complement each other to form a better-rounded, more useful learning intervention.

Unilever mLearning

By Ron Edwards

Unilever is exploring how networked mLearning on various platforms can support classroom delivery, blended learning, and performance support experiences, as well as being applied as internal viral marketing. This approach is part of its "be where the eyeballs are" strategy to better reach people in their moments of need and increase productivity during otherwise "down time" through access to content, tools, external experts, and one another.

Unilever launched several proof of concept PDA applications in 2003, which are creating excitement and interest in further developments. The following are some examples, the first three of which are produced by Apex Interactive (http://www.apexinteractive.co.uk):

Value Creation

Unilever utilizes a common methodology for assessing financial performance. The primary way to learn this is an online (Intranet)-based course, which often is used as a prerequisite for workshops where the concepts and terminology are applied. An analysis tool developed to support this was also produced for the iPAQ platform. This provides portability to instantly analyze opportunities and communicate these in real time. Leaders have been showing each other this new application and discussing further handheld tool ideas.

Code of Business Principles

Unilever implemented the Code of Business Principles globally through workshops and online learning. A reference guide with rich graphics and sound clips of leaders reinforcing key messages was produced for the iPAQ, and a text/graphics only version for the Palm platform is still the most ubiquitous across the enterprise. It is intended that the online and iPAQ versions will continue to be updated to keep the Code alive and fresh in minds. The goal is for handheld versions to be used as a decision support and reference tool, and will be distributed on all new PDAs.

The U1 Model: How Unilever Works

Unilever has a model with graphical representation of how it is organized by key processes. These processes are well documented and supported by workshops and Web-based tools. Having the model available on the iPAQ platform provides a tool for managers to communicate where and how they work and helps introduce more people to further explore the model and its community while promoting a common vocabulary. Initial response was very favorable with active exploration of how to use iPAQs as a primary delivery platform. Video and audio clips of thought leaders and implementers are being added to make it a more compelling marketing tool.

Design for Excellence

Unilever runs a product design workshop in partnership with Viadynamics that helps teams and individuals creatively and quickly innovate with the consumer experience at the forefront. A short video of the weeklong experience was produced with voice-over to communicate the journey, in an effort to bring it to life for potential participants, enroll more teams in the learning process, and get the right mix of participants. This was optimized for playback on the iPAQ to serve as a viral marketing tool, and is produced by Viadynamics http://www.viadynamics.com.

Having explored numerous case studies of mLearning at the sales, services, and business process/performance levels, we now turn the focus of the book to learning theories related to mobile development.

Chapter Seven:
Instructional Design Principles for Wireless Development

Introduction to ISD Innovations for mLearning

By its very nature, anytime, anyplace learning assumes that the learner starts with a need and a motivation for some information that will help him or her perform an immediate action. We have discussed this performance-support orientation to thinking about mobile learning in previous areas of the book, but it merits restating here.

The essential modes of work when someone is mobile change and become very self-directed and communicative. Accessing knowledge bases and communicating with people who have knowledge become core functions.

The following section will highlight several key information design and instructional design models that may prove effective for your mobile solutions. It is critical to emphasize the fundamental difference between information design and instructional design. Both are important to the development of sound instructional content—particularly for mobile, which has size and operational constraints that take some time to get used to.

Anecdotes from the Field

From some of our earliest development efforts with mobile, we began to see that certain design guidelines were necessary and important. The first project that we did on a Palm PDA proved to be challenging for several reasons. First, we did not know if people would learn using these small devices. As mentioned before, the thought of taking a course on a small screen with limited space and the usual time-sensitive pressures of being mobile did not seem particularly appealing on a personal level. I was reluctant to force something like this on our learners.

We set some early design goals around these thoughts, which include the following. Modules should be very short and follow a rather structured information design flow for easy navigation and familiarity. Interface, navigation, and controls should be consistent with the normal operating conventions of the devices. Finally, learning content should be built according to standards and, if possible, reusable in or from other formats.

As an example, the IP Troubleshooting Guide that we reviewed in the services case studies section earlier in the book was initially built for the Palm platform. Using the standard PQA (Palm Query Application) format allowed us to follow the user interface and operating conventions with which learners who had Palms would already be familiar. This allows the learner to transcend thinking about the interface and get right to the business of learning or gathering information.

Additionally, we wanted to structure the information in an easy-to-find information design structure. Both the IP Troubleshooting Guide and the 3Com Learning Assistant follow a model for information design called the inverted pyramid, commonly found in newspaper writing. It begins by providing an appropriate title followed by an overview that gives the core message, which is then followed up with progressively deeper levels of detail. When space is at a premium and people sometimes just need the base overview on a topic, this method works well. Learners can always click again to get more information using this model.

Another useful convention has to do with predictability of the format and structure of information. For example, with the 3Com Learning Assistant, the flow of information for each product or topic is always: Introduction, Benefits, Features, and Specifications. This four-page model has predictability that allows for easier navigation and information flow as the learner goes deeper into each topic.

In order to effectively size the information chunks that make up this well-designed information flow, it was also necessary to change the thinking of our instructional and information designers. When we first started creating performance modules for the Palm, we took a standard 3" × 5" index card and used this as our model and size guide for information. To the extent possible, information should be structured and chunked to fall within this card model. (I was amazed how small some people could write when necessary.) We also began to see a shift in thought process to a concise performance-oriented briefing rather than exhaustive information. A Cliff's Notes or cheat sheet style of summary, recipe, and tips began to emerge.

After completing the PDA version of the IP Troubleshooting Guide, we tried our hand at a version that would operate on a smart phone. The WAP (WML) version again conformed to the interface conventions of the device, but presented significantly larger challenges as the screen size decreased. In addition to more difficult user input through a numeric keypad interface, the smaller format and resolution screens coupled with the variety in line spacing and screen density made coming up with standard conventions more difficult. In the end, writing to the lowest common denominator proved effective.

Another information design technique that proved useful in getting our IDs and ISDs thinking along the right size ranges was to take the same 3" × 5" index card from our PDA example and cut it into quarters. This then became the size standard for smart phone screens. It also conformed to the information convention of WML called "stacks," because in essence that is what you had after the design process—stacks of interlinked mini cards.

The team has since gone to a much more sophisticated toolset, including a database driven storyboarding form that has a character and word guideline and limit as well as graphical conventions and formats.

These design guidelines can serve as heuristics for your development efforts and should start you down an appropriate path. The next sections will further explore design models and concepts. Information design and instructional design are intermixed in these examples, as the two go hand-in-hand in most cases.

Instructional Development Shifts

In order to fully capitalize on the promise of wireless for learning, a fundamental shift in learning model, style, and application must occur. The shift from a training orientation to a performance support orientation is an important overall framework change.

By its nature, this shift demands new learning models focused on just-in-time, just-in-place models. It is characterized by short learning segments that can be measured in seconds rather than hours. The information or exercises should be available instantly and may not follow the standard format of objective definition, content delivery, and assessment or practice. Context of need defines the objective (I must complete the task before me; that is my objective in the learning exercise or procedure review). The assessment of learning is validated in the real world through the successful completion of the task at hand.

Is it good training? Probably not. Is it good performance support? Maybe. Can you learn and perform better through this? Yes. Is this the most efficient use of the technology based on its current features and limitations? You bet!

User Interface Shifts

If those infrastructure issues weren't enough, you must also consider the technical side of your content distribution on small devices. Not only do you have a much smaller screen size, but that size is not consistent across platforms; neither is your color depth or text formats.

To take a first pass at this dilemma, designers should consider how much information will be on a typical screen. The jury is still out on what the optimal amount of text, graphics (if any), or combination works best, but a rule of thumb that we have been using when considering the PDA-sized devices like Palm and PocketPC size is to use a 3" × 5" index card as the maximum amount of information that can be on a page. For smart phones, cut this into four and you have something logical.

Learner Experience Shifts

Some of the most fundamental changes I would convey to you come from my own anecdotal experience using wireless and handheld devices to augment my learning. Note that we intentionally use the term *augment my learning* because one of the fundamental shifts in thinking is away from the idea that wireless delivery system will be good for all types of learning, in all situations. The best examples of wireless delivery of eLearning are in conjunction with another delivery method like Web-based training modules or as performance support after a live training event.

Designing for short instances of learning that are self-directed will be a norm for these new devices. A "kitchen sink" design philosophy will most certainly fail because it violates the new paradigm for instant access and short sessions that are familiar to frequent handheld device users. It also stretches the technical limits of these less robust devices, making it harder to develop.

I admire developers who go with the paradigm of the device and conform to the normal user conventions. For instance, instead of trying to cram a course delivery system, class scheduling agent, and testing system into one large application, breaking these out into logical, separate components will help learners make better use of your tools.

Details of the Instructional Design Model for mLearning and Wireless Performance Support

Several techniques that are well-grounded in theory and research serve as guiding design principles for delivering content to handhelds. The main models for delivery of wireless learning and performance content spring from the research of Gloria Gery in Performance Support and David Jonassen in Constructivism.

Performance Support addresses the needs of individuals for information and instruction while on the job. One of the key functions of mobile computing is the ability to take applications with you to a remote place of work. The ability to access work instructions, real-time information, and other features are key components in reaching the promise of just-in-time, just-in-place, just-enough learning.

Usually, you would not send a totally untrained technician or salesperson out in the field alone. Some level of existing experience, knowledge, or expertise is assumed in order for an individual to be trusted to do a job. With this in mind, the idea of constructivism—which states that the learner should be given a good roadmap and the freedom to build their own path through the learning based on their needs—is the second guiding instructional theory that will help instructional designers better understand the differences in developing for this new medium, which has very distinct audience characteristics and content types.

For example, a searchable database with all of the error codes for a particular device could be a powerful interface to find what you need, when you need it. While this may not be training, it is learning and is definitely a performance improvement function.

These two guiding design models manifest themselves throughout the development process as decisions about audience, use, content, and context are made. The following section highlights key decision points and processes for developing instructions.

Details of the Instructional Design Process for mLearning

In the tradition of blended eLearning, most of our projects to date have treated wireless as a branch off of the core development trunk for design of a full asynchronous Web-based training course. As such, the design process has been similar, but we have noted a few distinctions worth mentioning.

In each phase of a traditional ADDIE (Analysis, Design, Development, Implementation, and Evaluation) development process, there are differences worth pointing out. One area that becomes even more important is the beginning phase that is often overlooked in this model: planning. Upfront planning takes on a whole new importance when you are required to deliver learning content to different devices for different uses, in different environments or contexts.

Understanding the usage can help you go a long way in making decisions during the other phases of development. If you know you might be delivering to a handheld or wireless device before you begin development, you can make effective decisions that cut down on redesign time and prepare the materials for multi-format delivery in advance. This allows you to work off of the same base of content and reformat it with a minimum of expense. An example will give us the best grounding in reality for this abstract thought process.

Constructivism

From the case studies you saw, many early examples of mLearning repurposed course modules that we built using an objectivist model that stated the objectives; delivered information around those objectives; and validated or reinforced this information. With mobile content, the context is critically important as is your level of experience with similar concepts.

In many of the areas we work in, we deal with experts who learn constantly. They are self-directed, and the thought of being sent to training or forced to go through a course module can be quite distasteful (or a form of punishment).

The fundamental tenant of constructivism is to allow learners who understand their context and know (to some degree) what they need to learn to build their own paths through learning material. It is also sometimes called discovery learning.

This model is particularly well suited for performance-oriented mobile learning since it streamlines the overall learning process. Because the learner starts with an immediate need to locate, recall, or further learn something, this becomes the implied learning objective. For example, the learner must use a search function to locate information on a revised invoicing procedure; once the item has been located, reviewed, and executed, the successful transaction serves as a means of authentic assessment as to the effectiveness of both the performance support and the learner's ability to perform the task.

In essence, all that must be delivered via mobile technology is an interface to locate the material (e.g., navigation buttons, concept map, or search field) and a consistent shell and format to deliver the material (e.g., text procedures, graphics, rich media). The learning objectives are implied and the assessment is externally achieved through accomplishment of the task, or merely finding and using the right content. An example of this model in action is the ability to search a database of known issues and return the results, as is the case in the IP Troubleshooting Guide.

There are many variations on the theme of constructivism. One other example is the use of concept maps to map out a knowledge domain (Novak, 1998; Spiro, Coulson, Feltovich, & Anderson, 1988).

Concept Map of a Balanced Diet

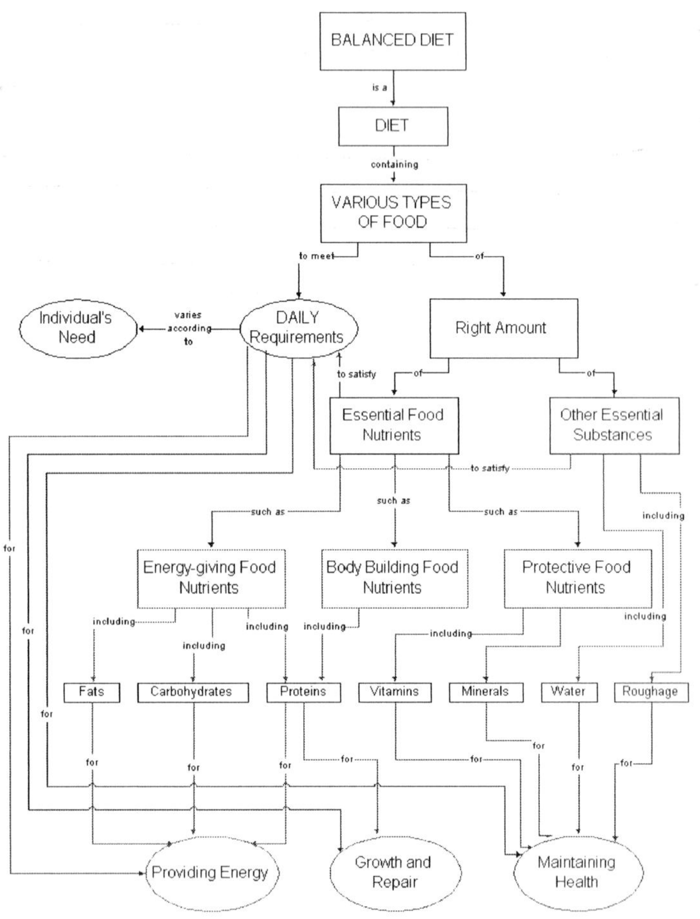

Source: From Biology Teaching Home Page, http://www.fed.cuhk.edu.hk/~johnson/misconceptions/concept_map/Balanced_diet.html)

These maps can be an interesting and useful navigation method, since elements can be hyperlinked to form a comprehensive, yet intelligible mesh of knowledge. Concept maps can also be a valid teaching method, because they require thorough understanding and synthesis of a diagram mapping the links between elements within a domain. An interesting, Palm-based tool for this is PICO Map from HiCE. This free tool allows the learner to build concept maps right on his or her Palm and then share them with other students or an instructor to validate understanding. This is an example of using constructivist techniques to learn something well, even if the subject is not generally known by the student. Joseph Novak of Cornell has even used these techniques effectively with elementary school children.

Collaborative Learning

One of the most exciting areas of innovation that has the most potential to grow over time is the use of handheld devices as collaborative tools. This makes sense considering the original purpose for building the devices: to connect people to people. Some of the latest technology that makes use of the e-911 system for location awareness and location services is now being used to connect people to each other on these handheld devices, whether through the latest craze of speed dating or expert location at a conference.

This is an exciting time to be looking at mobile devices for collaboration and connectivity of expertise to the people who have need for it. Services like Dodgeball (recently bought by Google), FindMy Friends from Cingular Wireless (formerly AT&T Wireless), and services like Groupvine and Ima Hima in Japan hold significant promise.

Considering Ima Hima, for example, users are taking advantage of this service for dating efforts. A person could see someone across the bar or restaurant who has a similar profile, interest, or hobby, and think, "Oh, a Japanese surfer. There are not many of those; I'll go over there and see what that's about!" Consider what rich dialogue could come as you start to find experts or people with similar interests to form communities, based both on location and on having that mobile connectivity to be able to get access to them right when you need them.

Instant Information Access

Having access to real-time information at your fingertips, with the instant-on capabilities or the always-on capabilities of any of these devices, opens up a world of opportunity not only for performance support, but for access to real-time data downloads for either enterprise systems or from learning resources. The notion of pushing information over a channel the same way e-mail is sent has not even begun to be explored to the depths and details that could produce breakthroughs in how we learn and in how we set up profiles to determine what information should be sent to us and when.

Grasping a context of what people need and getting them that information with a minimum amount of effort could have people getting digest information sent to them in e-mail of small short learning modules that they could go through in their spare, down, or wait time. Having real-time access to the information that you need in the field is what our case studies and examples, as well as the philosophy and learning theory behind looking at performance support, concentrate on.

As a hypothetical example, imagine your phone having some level of location awareness and a feature that sets up a profile, allowing you to turn it on in any city and automatically map some suggestions for food you might like to eat. If you have a travel itinerary set online, you could also have maps to locations such as hotels, rental car agencies, an organization's corporate location, and other local knowledge—all right at your finger tips.

All of this is an example of having access to information about your environment that is instantly available to you with minimal effort. You could follow that up with information from your enterprise systems about the client or organizations with whom you are meeting, along with information on their products and recent news reports—all in one discrete package that does not require you to concatenate information from four or five different sources and have access to that information after a long period of searching. This is a promise that mobility, converging with personal profiles and location awareness, hold out to us.

Conclusion

In conclusion, those who desire any-time, any-place learning need not be quickly scared off by the supposed limits of design and practicality. As this chapter has demonstrated, a creative, out-of-the-box approach can lead to the recovery of large chunks of time and the realization of additional revenues. We now move to a thorough discussion of current multimedia developments in the wireless world.

Chapter Eight: Multimedia Development for Mobile

Introduction

With all of our discussion so far surrounding rationale for mLearning, a performance-oriented model, and examples of simple but effective solutions, you might be wondering why there is a chapter devoted to multimedia.

In short, this is where a great deal of the promise of the future of mLearning is held. It also is important to understand the limitations of multimedia on mobile devices before over-promising or believing the hype. Finally, we want to take a current snapshot of the capabilities and tools you can use now or expect to see in the near future.

Principles

How do multimedia elements such as audio, video, animation, and sophisticated graphics fit into a performance-oriented model for mLearning? The main value of multimedia under this context is to further engage the learner by reinforcing text or (small) graphical elements with multisensory input that responds to the learner's preference and the best available method of presentation, based on the type of content being delivered.

For example, if you want someone to learn a very kinesthetic task such as setting a pressure gauge correctly, a very short, close-up video clip that shows the exact motion and steps can accomplish in seconds the same thing it would take many small pages of text to describe.

Another example depends on the learner's environment. If a learner is driving, it is a common practice to listen to books on tape or study a language. In this case, for auditory learners, there is an excellent opportunity to make use of their time in traffic without compromising safety or unduly dividing attention to the important task of driving.

Imagine having access to a whole library of content through an mLearning device (like Audible's audio players) or wireless transfer from a central database (like an XM satellite radio system educational "station"). You might even be able to access this information over a cellular network.

I have had significant success using this book-on-tape style content and learning method from an MP3 player with a large hard drive. I can store hundreds of hours of content and have an easy-to-access database of material that plays back through my car stereo system. These are examples of highly integrative multimedia uses and appropriate uses of the media for a defined audience, purpose, type of content, and environment.

Capabilities and Current Limitations

While I am quite excited about the growing capabilities of wireless technology and the integration of core multimedia capabilities (animation, complex graphics, audio, and video), I also am a realist when it comes to the limitations based on current technology. This must be factored in as you look at the various solutions. One more guiding principle that may help shape your view of the capabilities and limitations is the notion that just because it is available or can be done, does not mean that it should be done or is common practice.

For example, I can watch full-motion, streaming video on my PocketPC using PacketVideo over my WiFi WLAN card connection. The screen size is about what I get on my desktop machine since most video is 320 × 240 pixels. Some of you might be impressed that this is possible and really quite easy—but the amount of time I actually spend doing this versus using e-mail or Web services is minimal. The battery drain is great, and the technology including software requires some configuration. It is possible to do this, but is it practical?

I call this section capabilities and current limitations because many of the current limits are not necessarily technical or permanent. Let's take a look at limitations first. Some limitations are based on cost factors, installed populations that have equipment meeting the minimum requirements, and user/learner mindset. For example, I have heard many people say, "Yes, it is possible to take a rich media course using a PDA, but why?" or, "I'd go crazy trying to learn using that little screen and tiny controls." This context makes it more difficult to sell people on the idea that they should take courses that engage them with rich media, when there are physical limitations that are difficult for some people to get past.

Another serious limitation is bandwidth. In the Local Area Network (LAN), it is not as difficult of an issue since high-speed access to a wired network is available. For Wide Area Networking (WAN), the bandwidth is becoming available to support rich media through 3G networks, but it can be cost prohibitive for delivery of large blocks of data, typical of multimedia content.

Another limitation that is rapidly being overcome is processor speed and battery life. I lump these two together since the increase in processor speed usually causes more battery resource to be used. It is hard to find the right mix of speed to be able to run animations and video and battery life so that a substantial amount of usage time can be sustained.

As an example, I have watched full screen, half speed (15 frames per second) videos with sound for no longer than 3½ hours on my PocketPC (brand and name are withheld to protect the semi-innocent). I don't fault the manufacturers; this is just the price of heavy media use on these devices. Some would argue that 3½ hours is fine, but with other uses throughout the day, I can only use the device for half a day without thinking about recharging the battery or popping in another charged one. This is a lot of burden to put on a user who is not technology tolerant.

I may have scared some of you off with my description of the current limitations. If so, just consider that these are not permanent limitations and are changing rapidly. You should approach this with a sober view, but not all uses of multimedia and rich content are created equal. Some uses are truly worth it based on the learning models we explored previously. With that said, let's look at some of the capabilities in general.

Some people do not believe me when I tell them that it is possible to have rich animations, detailed graphics, full-screen video, and high-quality audio on mobile devices. This perception is rapidly changing with computer stores, phone manufacturers, and cellular network providers heavily marketing the capabilities and innovative uses.

The fact is that it is possible to review course materials on color Palm and PocketPC devices as well as play advanced games on color cell phones using Java technology. Camera phones allow playback of short video segments in very small formats. Capabilities on these devices will only continue to expand.

Tools that many computer users are quite familiar with are now available on PDAs and phones, and sometimes have even better integrated communication functions than desktop tools because of some devices' built-in wireless communication. Palm has picture viewers and Web browsers like Blazer for review of images and Web pages. Microsoft has ported a limited functionality version of its desktop Internet Explorer software to the PocketPC, called Pocket Internet Explorer (PIE). There is significant multimedia integration function available through the PocketPC 2002 or above versions that can link to Microsoft Media Player and pocket versions of the Office products.

Documents and media-rich eBooks can be viewed through several different readers including Microsoft Reader on PocketPC, Palm Reader (formerly Peanut Press), and multiplatform Adobe Acrobat for PalmOS or PocketPC. Macromedia Flash (animation, sound, and rich graphics integration) is available for PocketPC and Palm5 or above devices. There also are many specialized applications that allow you to integrate other advanced functions such as game engines in Java and Scalable Vector Graphics (SVG) to manipulate complex images and display them (great for engineering and CAD training).

Considering all of these generalities that describe capabilities of devices, let's take a look at some specific development and delivery tools and their capabilities.

Development

Tools in the development category are enabling technologies that allow developers to create learning applications and content. Some will seem familiar to the everyday user, while others will require somewhat of a learning curve.

HTML

In theory, any tool that can be used to write HTML (HyperText Markup Language) can be used to produce mobile learning content for delivery on a wide variety of devices. There are many similarities in writing WAP content for cell phones, Web Clipping Applications for Palms, and HTML for Microsoft Pocket Internet Explorer. It currently appears that HTML will continue to be a great equalizer across platforms, devices, software applications, and delivery systems on mobile devices, just as it has been on the desktop.

The reality is that certain tools are optimized for creating mobile content and reformatting existing Web data to fit the small screen. While a comprehensive list is beyond our scope, several example applications with specialized libraries for development of mobile Web content include Microsoft FrontPage and Macromedia DreamWeaver among others. Further listings will be available on this book's Web site in the future.

Beyond these, we will explore specific tools that take HTML or similar formats and convert the information to specific formats or for delivery to specific devices in the following sections of this chapter.

WAP

WAP (Wireless Application Protocol) is a standard data format that can be used on cell phones and other small format devices. It is a limited function, small format version of Web traffic, performing the same function as HTTP for the Web. The format for developing content pages is called WML (Wireless Markup Language).

If you remember Hypercard, where you had "stacks" of cards to produce a deck, then you will instantly understand the metaphor for WAP/WML. Multiple cards can be created as a flow and are all part of the same WML page. These pages can be created as simply as writing them in Notepad, but are typically created with a software development kit (SDK) that lets you test what you have written in a phone emulator, right on your computer screen. Many free SDKs are available from major phone manufacturers and industry groups. Nokia, Ericsson, and Motorola all have SDKs available.

I use all of these, but generally start my work in the OpenWave SDK since they are the original creators of the WAP standard. The current version can also be used to develop MMS and HTML content for mobile devices as well. The generic emulator simulates how your content should look, navigate, and operate across a wide range of cellular phones and devices. Some authoring tools also allow for creation of WAP content, such as the Macromedia DreamWeaver library for WAP development.

Authoring Tools

Next, we'll take a closer look at several authoring tools that might be useful to add to your developer's toolbox. These tools are particularly useful if you have developers who are already using the desktop versions. The switch to small device thinking, coupled with existing knowledge of the desktop tools, can produce rapid results with minimal programming knowledge. This allows you or your team to focus on content development rather than the complexities and technical aspects of mLearning.

Lectora

For those of you familiar with Lectora publisher, you will be right at home with either the Palm or PocketPC version. While the programs are completely unique to each other, there are some similar functions. Most notably, the templating function is quite similar between the three versions. Best of all, it is the same basic graphical user interface (GUI) that allows you to drag and drop elements onto your screens. Best of all, the price of the mobile versions are quite a bit less than the desktop version. For more information see http://www.lectora.com.

Adobe Acrobat

I'm sure many of you have heard of Adobe Acrobat as a de facto standard format for accurate document display and printing. The .pdf (portable document format) is quite prevalent in both publishing and Web delivery of documents. Most importantly, almost any file format that can be printed can be converted to Acrobat format. The document format is read by the Adobe Acrobat Reader and the corresponding Web plug-in.

The reason I am excited about the Acrobat format in the context of mLearning is that we currently have free Adobe Acrobat Readers for both the PalmOS and the PocketPC. With a simple reformatting, conversion, and synchronization process, it is possible to bring critical documents with you on your mobile devices. This means that many job aids, work instructions, and other performance support documents could be made available on handhelds with relative ease and very low cost. The most recent versions even have security functions so that published works are properly protected from mass duplication.

Specialized Platform Tools and Software Development Kits (SDKs)

A Software Development Kit (SDK) is a programming package that enables someone to develop applications for a specific platform. Typically an SDK includes one or more Application Program Interfaces (APIs), routines, programming tools, and documentation. SDKs offer a powerful, end-to-end platform upon which you can create your own digital media solutions that meet your personal or business needs.

Microsoft Mobile SDK

According to Microsoft, the market for mobile devices is growing rapidly; analysts predict by 2008 there will be more than 100 million converged devices and 2 billion mobile phone subscribers. This creates an exciting opportunity for developers who want to build innovative applications with Windows Mobile, Microsoft's SDK for products such as the PocketPC and Smart Phone. The former facilitates the mobile use of such Microsoft standards as Word, Internet Explorer, Outlook, and Excel, along with Reader. The new Microsoft Mobile Version 5 offers tools, APIs, and technologies for both native and managed application developers.

Palm WCA

When Palm Computing released the Palm VII, it introduced a Web application format called Web Clipping Applications (WCAs), also known as Palm Query Applications (PQAs). These terms are synonymous. PQAs are written in a subset of HTML 3.2, with a handful of special metadata tags and a few other conventions. A proxy server at the wireless service provider's site translates them into PQA format. PQAs are actually Palm record databases, with each page and image stored as a separate record. Web-enabled Palms are equipped with an internal application, called a Web clipper that reads the PQAs.

PQAs are typically built so that all static elements of a page reside on the handheld, while dynamic content is updated from the Internet. This approach minimizes the amount of data being sent across the slow wireless network. Unfortunately, PQAs cannot be installed wirelessly. The applications must be downloaded to the PDA using Palm's HotSync tool when the device is tethered to a PC. While this approach may be phased out, some of the early development principles still apply to good design and can serve as a pattern for effective usability.

Nokia, Ericsson, and Motorola SDKs and Emulators

The cellular manufacturers Nokia, Ericsson, and Motorola have also made their own SDKs available. Nokia's "Culture of Mobility" pages on its Web site help educate users on the big-picture possibilities of wireless applications and devices. Ericsson Mobility World offers remote testing services over the Internet and end-to-end verification with a mobile phone and radio network at one of Ericsson's test centers. Motorola's Web site allows users to download all the latest tools and resources to create J2ME Applications, which are discussed in the next section.

Java BREW/J2ME

Java is a high-level programming language developed by Sun Microsystems. Small Java applications, called Java applets, can be downloaded from a Web server and run on a computer by a Java-compatible browser such as Netscape Navigator and Microsoft Internet Explorer.

Short for Java 2 Platform Micro Edition, J2ME is Java's wireless device platform, also known as Java BREW (Binary Runtime Environment for Wireless), allowing developers to use a toolkit to create applications and programs for wireless and mobile devices.

J2ME consists of two elements, configurations, and profiles. Configurations provide a set of libraries and a virtual machine for a category of wireless device. There are two configurations for J2ME, one for fixed wireless devices and one for mobile wireless devices. Profiles are APIs built on top of configurations to provide a run-time environment for a specific device, such as a PDA or cell phone.

RIM Blackberry Java Tools

Development for the Blackberry devices from Research in Motion (RIM) is slightly different from the other development tools and techniques we've examined, but probably shows the most in common with the Java Brew and J2ME's Micro Edition development found with smart phones. Blackberry has a Java development environment, or JDE, that sits on top of the J2ME platform and allows developers to build Java applications that are delivered on their mobile devices.

RIM has a development site at http://www.blackberry.com. It includes free SDKs and detailed instructions on getting started and where to find the other Java development resources for free that you will need to build out components. This holds a great deal of promise particularly for the financial community, which has embraced the Blackberry wholeheartedly, and for other groups that have found the Blackberry to be one of the devices of choice for their activities.

Macromedia Flash

Flash is a relatively bandwidth-friendly and browser-independent vector-graphic animation technology that allows users to draw their own animations or import other vector-based images. Macromedia Flash MX 2004 allows designers and developers to integrate video, text, audio, and graphics into immersive, rich experiences that deliver superior results for interactive marketing and presentations, eLearning, and application user interfaces.

Flash is used by more than one million professionals and offers a lightweight, cross-platform run time engine that can be used not just for rich media, but also for enterprise applications, communications, and mobile applications. Flash 8 Professional includes a mobile emulator that allows a user to instantly preview content across 90 different handsets.

Delivery

Now that we have examined the development tools, let's look at some of the most prominent delivery tools.

Flash Lite

Macromedia Flash Lite is a new profile of Macromedia Flash Player that is designed specifically for mobile phones. This new profile was needed, according to Macromedia, because mass-market phones do not have sufficient processing power and memory to support the entire Flash Player 7 feature set while supporting unique requirements such as network connectivity. Macromedia says it is continuing to create profiles for other key device categories such as interactive television set top boxes and PDAs.

Pocket Internet Explorer (PIE)

A mobile version of Microsoft Internet Explorer, Pocket Internet Explorer (PIE) allows users to view either Web or WAP pages on their Windows Mobile–based device. While browsing, you can also download new files and programs from the Internet. A full-featured Internet browser, PIE is optimized for devices with small, vertically oriented displays and for cached or customized content.

HTML functionality is equivalent to that of Microsoft Internet Explorer version 3.2, with support for tables, forms, and frames. A fit-to-screen option dynamically resizes Web pages to maximize viewing on handheld devices without requiring the user to scroll across a page. A Zoom menu option allows the user to view text on the screen in different sizes.

Automatic state detection determines whether the device is connected to the Internet and, if not, diverts the browser to a cached version of the Web page. On Microsoft Windows CE .NET-based devices that include Microsoft ActiveSync®, users can update their cached Web pages automatically by designating a Web page displayed on their desktop machine as a mobile favorite. Then, whenever the mobile device is synchronized to the desktop machine, the current version of that page is downloaded to PIE.

There are similar Web browsers available on almost every platform from other vendors, but Microsoft has a strong presence and a forward thinking approach for multimedia integration.

Microsoft Windows Media Player

Microsoft's Windows Media Player 10 gives users more music and choices than previous versions, and for the first time makes it possible to synchronize high-quality music, video, and photos to the latest portable devices. The product's built-in Digital Media Mall provides a large selection of music and video stores, allowing options such as buying music downloads, signing up for a music subscription, or renting a movie.

Audible

Audible provides digital audio entertainment and information. Users can choose from more than 25,000 best-selling digital audiobooks, radio shows, audio versions of popular magazines, daily newspapers, and more. The programming can be downloaded and listened to using devices such as iPod®, Palm OS handheld, Pocket PC, Creative® MuVo®, PC, Mac, or on CDs you burn. Audible uses security technologies, including encryption, to protect purchased programs, preventing a user from being able to convert its formats to MP3.

Vector Graphics

Adobe Acrobat's Scalable Vector Graphics (SVG) is a new graphics file format and Web development language that enables Web developers and designers to create dynamically generated, high-quality graphics from real-time data with precise structural and visual control. SVG developers can create a new generation of Web applications based on data-driven, interactive, and personalized graphics.

SVG is text based and works seamlessly with current Web technologies like HTML, GIF, JPEG, PNG, SMIL, ASP, JSP, and JavaScript. Graphics created in SVG can be scaled without loss of quality across various platforms and devices. SVG can be used on the Web, in print, and even on portable devices while retaining full quality.

Conclusion

While this short list can only begin to describe the plethora of current delivery options (and those coming in the future), it is a good representation to get you started. Today's multimedia capabilities for mLearning have only begun to scratch the surface. Advancements will continue to integrate existing programs into functional and helpful mobile uses, and new strides in this arena will quickly help more people assimilate themselves—as both learners and producers of content—into this emerging lifestyle. Next, our discussion will shift to the integration of business and learning functions in a variety of settings.

Chapter Nine:
The Integration of Wireless Learning and Performance Support into Other Core Function Wireless Initiatives

Introduction

In this chapter, we will discuss how learning and performance come together for crucial functions that enable a company to serve its clients in a variety of mobile capacities. We begin with a focus on strategic ways of managing information in order to make mobile as practical and cost-effective as possible.

Links to CRM (Customer Relationship Management)

Significant cost savings for a project can be realized with a decidedly systems-based approach to injecting learning and performance support into your mobile and wireless efforts. Much of the "heavy lifting" that would otherwise be attempted via a handheld unit can be done at the service side or back end of the infrastructure side.

Instead of loading sophisticated databases, processing, storage, and warehousing on a small handheld device that was never meant to accommodate these, you can handle this information through a server. The information is automatically processed and formatted for the handheld unit. Even well-equipped PDAs struggle with information overload, and imagine the challenge of trying to engineer very sophisticated data processes on mobile phones and small, low processor-speed devices.

As we explore taking mobile to the next level, with even smaller devices that facilitate the point solutions or provide personal data or information management, we encounter deeper levels of need for offloading the local processing to remote units.

Again, a systems approach will save significant time, money, and aggravation—both on the part of the developer and the end user, the customer—when allowing each device, network, tool, and process to function at its best in a larger enterprise initiative or even for point-of-service solutions.

Customer Relationship Management (CRM) is an integrated approach to identifying, acquiring, and retaining customers in accordance with this philosophy of remote data storage and flow. "By enabling organizations to manage and coordinate customer interactions across multiple channels, departments, lines of business, and geographies, CRM helps organizations maximize the value of each customer interaction and drive superior corporate performance" (Webopedia, 2005).

Today's organizations must manage customer interactions across multiple communications channels—including the Web, call centers, field sales, and dealers or partner networks. Many organizations also have multiple lines of business with many overlapping customers.

The challenge is to make it easy for customers to do business with the organization any way they want—at any time, through any channel, in any language or currency—and to make customers feel that they are dealing with a single, unified organization that recognizes them at every touch point.

Siebel and Oracle

Siebel and Oracle are two companies heavily involved in CRM.

"The benefits of CRM are clear: By streamlining processes and providing sales, marketing, and service personnel with better, more complete customer information, CRM enables organizations to establish more profitable customer relationships and decrease operating costs," Siebel Systems (2005) states on its Web site. "Sales organizations can shorten the sales cycle and increase key sales-performance metrics such as revenue per sales representative, average order size, and revenue per customer. Marketing organizations can increase campaign response rates and marketing-driven revenue while simultaneously decreasing lead-generation and customer-acquisition costs. Customer service organizations can increase service-agent productivity and customer retention while decreasing service costs, response times, and request-resolution times" (Siebel Systems, 2005).

Within the company, Siebel Sales helps organizations grow revenues more quickly, predictably, and profitably by helping organizations focus on the right deals at the right time. Siebel Quote & Order Lifecycle Management supports complex pricing and product configuration, quote approval, availability checking, and credit and payment verification to ensure customer orders are complete, valid, and accurate. Siebel Call Center and Service applications support end-to-end, closed-loop service and enable organizations to increase service profitability, reduce cost per contact, optimize resource management, and enhance customer satisfaction and loyalty.

Oracle's integrated CRM solution is a set of applications that provide information-driven sales, service, and marketing. It is built on an open, standards-based architecture that streamlines business processes, improves data quality, and allows all of an organization's key divisions to draw from the same source of data.

Oracle offers more than 50 CRM-specific applications, ranging from precisely measuring marketing campaigns to automatically dispatching field technicians to remote locations. Its E-Business Suite 11i.10 offers more than 2,600 enhancements to Oracle applications, including expanded marketing resource management and campaign management.

SimplexGrinnell and Valero Energy

An example of effective services comes from SimplexGrinnell Fire and Security and some of its pilot projects that provide audio and handheld mobile access to CRM data. The ability to link this important services information to fire safety tips; trouble-shooting questions and answers through a voice mail–like recording and message retrieval system; and important messages for management can all be done through this audio box type of approach. This is even achieved in a decidedly low-tech way by maximizing the use and benefits of many existing voice mail systems that are in operation today.

When taken a step further and adding interactive voice response and access to data from a handheld unit, such CRM aspects can be instrumental in meeting the business objectives of services organizations. This can lead to automation of key processes, such as SimplexGrinnell's inspections and equipment reviews and follow-up on services and sales needs, identifying issues for long-term excellent customer support and service.

We will discuss SimplexGrinnell in more depth in the next chapter. But if such services can shave seconds or minutes off of the process, give better data quality, and speed up customer service—and therefore lead to customer satisfaction—then there are many ample reasons at a strategic level for initiatives that involve wireless technology and devices with elements of learning and performance support.

The Valero Energy case study we discussed in Chapter 5 is another good example of integrating performance support and documentation into the quality inspection processes, as well as the online forms that can be synchronized into a local desktop or sent wirelessly. This allows a person to have access to necessary information at his or her fingertips while performing field services tasks in a plant setting.

These examples have been intended to get you thinking about how you might integrate your own existing enterprise systems or high level strategic initiatives.

Mobile Augmented Reality: Symbol University Handheld Learning Assistant

Some of the latest research out of MIT and the military is finding its way into the commercial sector to benefit mobile workers. The principles of augmented reality—an emerging discipline that combines virtual reality, simulations and performance support with real-world activities and objects—give learners the best of both "worlds" in an action learning setting.

Henry Jenkins (2004) of MIT describes augmented reality as "...heightening our awareness of the real world by annotating it with information conveyed by mobile technologies. *Augmented* reality has powerful new applications for education, tourism, and storytelling." The novel use of handheld devices allows for location-aware learning that is driven by the context of a learner's work environment. Scenarios become more realistic, and performance support is provided within the flow of work.

Opportunity

Symbol Technologies has a new series of handheld devices (PPT8000) that allows augmented reality principles to be implemented. Symbol commissioned RWD Technologies to develop a prototype module that could make use of advanced features such as built-in Microsoft's Pocket Internet Explorer Web browser, Macromedia Flash support, barcode scanning, image processing, WiFi, and next generation RFID (Radio Frequency IDentifier) support. These features enable some of Symbol's top clients to modernize work processes and enable their workforces through mobile technology. Adding an element of learning and performance support further enhances skills and efficiencies of people involved in complex business processes.

Setting

To provide the broadest example of use, a work flow from the pharmaceutical manufacturing and distribution industries was selected by Symbol University. Wes Wisham, Senior Business Development Manager for Symbol Technologies EMEA, states, "It is important for us to provide a realistic scenario to show how the advanced device capabilities could be used to promote learning integrated with the work that is typically completed using our world-class handheld devices."

The prototype module centers on three distinct task groupings in an overall process flow. Integrating the learning into the workflow is a critical element in this leading-edge solution.

The sections are as follows:

1. Access control
   a. Real-time training certification
2. Quality inspection learner support
3. Inventory and shipping
   a. Product info and performance support
   b. RFID tracking and task automation

Imagine walking into a pharmaceutical manufacturing and storage environment. You scan your badge with the barcode reader, and the handheld unit "knows" who you are. Next, you scan a small barcode on the doorframe or enter a serial number. Your access levels are then looked up and determined. If you are certified to work in the environment, you may enter; if not, you must complete a real-time certification process to bring your records into compliance. Access control is only the beginning of a learning-integrated workflow environment.

Understanding how location-aware learning is integrated into other business processes can speed up work processes and improve performance. For example, quality inspection reports can be enhanced by providing integrated performance support and an easy-to-use workflow that is human-centered rather than system-centered.

Another step in the workflow is the task of reviewing inventoried items and shipping them. As an item's UPC code or other warehouse tracking code is scanned or input, the worker now has access to a full database of information about each product. This depth of content guarantees that a worker can make decisions based on much more information. This product information at your fingertips is performance support at its best.

Once the product is selected from inventory, shipping can begin. Currently, information about an item's physical location can be provided at each transfer station along the way. With the newest RFID capabilities, it is possible to track packages at any point, in real-time if needed. Access to information and knowledge immediately begins to link learning to the real world of work and operations in exciting new ways.

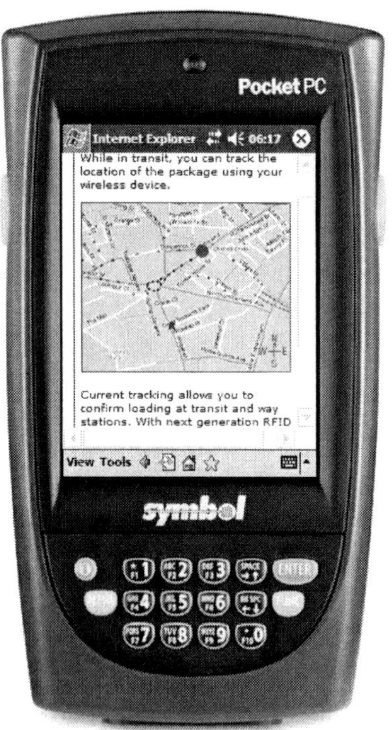

Results

Based on the encouraging feedback of both Symbol Technologies management and key customers, the demonstration module provides a design framework for integrating learning into the real world of work through leading-edge research like augmented reality. "Understanding the potential for the technology and the location-aware learning processes will open new uses for our devices and help our customers do their jobs better," states Wes Wisham of Symbol University. "Based on our initial reference design, we look forward to what the future of mobile learning holds."

Conclusion

As we have seen, mobile technology plays a crucial role in deepening opportunities for companies to more effectively serve their customers. Next, we will examine some options, such as synchronization, for mobile, on-the-go professionals before turning to our final focus with a look at the emerging future of mobile.

Chapter Ten: Other Options for Mobile Professionals

Let us briefly look at two mobile trends—one a few years old but still developing and one fairly cutting edge—that are of benefit to professionals constantly on the go. The first is synchronization for off-line use of content, even when no wireless connection is available. The second is voice-based access to data content. This pushes the boundaries of speech recognition and playback of recorded and computer-generated materials. Before we get ahead of ourselves, let's examine synchronization in more detail.

Synchronization

In the early days, we started discussing wireless learning, but found this was really a misnomer as we started to explore other ways you can get your learning on the go. The term mobile learning, or mLearning, emerged from this process.

One of the key technical disciplines that has been around much longer than wireless, which served to really promote this type of learning model, is synchronization. Synchronization allows you to have your data consistently at both a local connection, such as a desktop PC, and through a cable wire or other accessory connected to your handheld device, cell phone, or other portable. This notion of synchronization is useful when discussing the high price of having a data connection that's live all the time versus only having it available at certain times or just in a local office setting.

Fundamental to the understanding of mobile learning is realizing that it doesn't all have to be wireless or provide ready access to the Internet at all times; it only has to have it at the right time. When we start to look at our technology hierarchy, we find that sometimes data does not change on such a frequent basis that it has to be updated more than once a day or even a couple times per week. If that's the case, and the data is not that dynamic or changing all the time, it's very possible to synchronize the data you'll use the most and need while on the go without having to incur the high costs of a wireless connection.

This was one of the key features and selling points of the early Palm. The Palm Pilot had a one-button synchronization back to the desktop for all the records of an individual's schedules, address books, and other data files and notes that needed to be synchronized. With the more recent Palm additions of e-mail synchronization, access to local databases, and updating of those databases, the user has a powerful way of connecting and keeping data handy for use while on the road even without a wireless connection. Even with those devices that do have a wireless connection, it often is more efficient from a speed and processing standpoint to have the one-button synchronization that will keep your information up to date—and also backed up in case of loss, theft, or battery drain that can cause substantial loss of data or access to it.

A good example of synchronization in real-world action is the 3Com example we explored in our case study chapters. You might recall that 3Com had already ceded the market with Palms distributed to retail outlets such as Best Buy, Circuit City, CompUSA, and so forth. However, these Palms did not have wireless connections, a rather expensive upgrade. The company focused instead on synchronizing the data, automatically sending updates to the handheld devices, as a viable strategy to keep such information at the fingertips of retail sales agents without additional burdens to them or expenses to the store and 3Com.

Examining business objectives and resources is vital to understanding how a company can best leverage mobile technology and maybe save itself some money by not having to leverage wireless technology. Synchronization is a key means for doing this.

Many other systems, such as AvantGo, have made their name in synchronization of mobile content. Whether it involves caching of Web pages or access to Internet data, a synchronization strategy can offer periodic updates each time there is someone at a local desk who wants to synchronize.

Adobe Acrobat is another example of a system that does synchronization, as well as a data transform between synchronizations. This is a vital part of getting relevant data from a desktop with, for example, a Windows computing format, into the format suitable for a handheld. Even the Windows operating system and Windows CE, which for mobile devices is often called the Pocket PC platform, are not 100 percent compatible from a data standpoint. There are data transform and file extension changes that must happen in order for data to be usable on the local device. As time passes, there should be more and more of a change allowing the same formats supported on desktop machines to be supported on handheld machines, whether a cell phone, Pocket PC, Palm, or other PDA. Understanding synchronization is a key to understanding another tool in the toolbox of mobile technologies and, in this case, mLearning.

Voice-based Access

One of the newest tools worth exploring here is voice input integrated with data. This dynamic has perplexed some of the best technologists in the world who have wrestled with the conundrum of getting a device to function not as two parallel paths—with data as one channel and audio as the other—but to pull both functions together and operate well.

RWD Technologies won one of its eLearning Excellence Awards for an experiment performed for Tyco's SimplexGrinnell Fire and Security Division, which handles sprinkler head and fire suppression systems for buildings located across the world. Based on the type of work and the pace, it was unfeasible that sales and service personnel would spend a lot of time typing onto a small keyboard, so we examined what would be practical mobile applications for this division.

Realizing that the Fire Safety employees used voice response systems, we built a voice base portal that allowed them to access not only learning material, but Customer Relationship Management (CRM) data. Using the voice system, they could press "1" for more information on what they'd sold to certain clients; "2" for the fire safety tip of the day; "3" for the ability to hear some of the common problems clients were experiencing; and "4" to record a problem that they'd seen, which would then flow into a database for the most common problems. Another press of the button could present a message from the company CEO.

For example, the first option could tell one of the division's salespersons that five fire extinguishers were sold to ACME on a certain date at a certain price. This could be followed by the recorded fire safety tip of the day from the head of training. This voice data effectively reduces some of the sales rep's "windshield" time without having to take his or her eyes off the road or hands off the wheel.

The SimplexGrinnell reps also had the choice of having such sales data sent to their e-mail so that it could be at their desktop when they arrived back at the office and also immediately received on their mobile device. This saves the salesperson from having to remember something that could have been a very complex order, such as 20 fire extinguishers, fire panels, and so forth, with all the prices and numbers. This integration of voice and data gives the sales rep additional competitive power because the two elements work seamlessly together.

Technology is just now starting to catch up to such capabilities. We see these sorts of fusions coming in the future, and voice-based access is an exciting integration of voice and data.

Considering the future of mobile uses and mLearning, let us now turn to emerging trends as we close our study together.

Chapter Eleven: mLearning Implications for Next Generation Technologies

So what can we expect from the next generation of mLearning?

Exciting areas of location-aware learning, augmented reality, mobile collaboration, mobile gaming and simulation, and expert location await us. These are joined by richer use of media; decision support tools; and deeper access into enterprise systems and elements of performance support. These have a much more robust capability on the back end server side of the equation, and provide an elegant, small, and simplified subset of information on the handheld device itself.

During our final sections, we will take a look in greater detail at these opportunities and other areas of interest. We will also explore new devices and new device categories, such as the emerging handtop computer market and personal media players, along with other compelling mobile technologies.

Collaboration

The implications of the technology we have been discussing could lead to significant collaborative efforts, especially at conferences or other group events. Consider for a moment how many people you pass at such venues or sit next to who may possess common interests. Then, imagine getting an alert that you could either acknowledge or ignore each time you are in the same room as someone who is interested in mLearning. This could spark new conversations and knowledge sharing, especially in shy cultures.

Another significant opportunity for learning is the collaboration allowed by convergent devices. This includes access to shared information repositories; unified messaging systems; instant messages (or SMS); discussion boards; and of course e-mail. Recently in the United States, location-based services have shown great potential for collaboration. Because of the personal, mobile nature of the devices, it is possible to locate and identify colleagues and others with common interest to ask questions or begin a dialogue. Of course this must be a permission-based system, but it could produce a whole new way to collaborate or begin sharing knowledge.

As mentioned in Chapter Seven, an example that already is in use is the DoCoMo-based solution called Ima Hima. This service allows you to enter a profile, including keywords and interests. When you are in proximity of someone else who has similar interests, a signal is sent letting participants know that someone with a common interest or similar profile is nearby. At this point, the user can opt to send a short message to introduce him- or herself or find out more. If the user is confident that a good dialogue or match of interest could ensue, a phone call could be initiated to talk more or a meeting place could be established. Dodgeball (now owned by Google) is another location-aware tool for telling you where to locate experts, friends, or people with whom you may want to meet, and another one with perhaps more popular name recognition is AT&T Wireless's (now Cingular) Find My Friends.

Other forms of collaboration are becoming commonplace. Discussion boards and e-mail lists are quite common and easy to use from wireless devices.

The Convergence of Voice, Data, and Motion Images

A significant trend we will see with the rollout of 3G and 4G technologies (broadband, high-speed wireless) is the convergence of voice and data, and eventually video or moving images. This process is already underway with new device and service rollouts such as the popular Pocket PC phones like the Siemens and Toshiba models, and Palm-based phones like those from Samsung, PalmOne, and Kyocera.

All of these devices combine voice/audio/data/text and graphics, and in some cases even moving images/video and animations. Nokia and Samsung have released phones with a VGA 640 × 480 still image camera built in, and other makers have an attachable camera for sending images and collaborating. Some cameras with even greater resolutions have been announced. These devices hold the promise of opening up many new learning opportunities and the use of advanced media for collaboration.

However, capability does not necessarily ensure success. As these devices become more complex, there is great potential for "creeping featurism" that is not necessarily useful. Additionally, few convergent devices have succeeded in the past because of fears that one component breaking means repair or replacement of the whole device. (Think about your scanner, copier, printer, and fax combination devices—failure of one neutralizes the others.) This is a significant area of concern, with Gartner Group reporting an average of $4,100 per user each year for support of wireless devices (Gartner, 2005).

Another concern is the diminished battery life related to much greater power draws. Most convergent devices are promising similar battery life to that of regular cellular phones because of advanced battery technologies.

In addition, we have heard many people state, "Why are they (phone makers and cellular carriers) adding all these other features when they should really be focused on voice quality and coverage so that we can make a call from inside my home or office?"

In spite of these areas of concern, we are quite optimistic about the potential for learning and other core functions that can be accessed through these devices. A majority of technology-oriented individuals report wanting a single communication platform to minimize upkeep (multiple phonebooks and programs), travel burden, and complexity of managing multiple devices.

In the same way that voice, data, and moving image capabilities are being integrated, learning interventions that incorporate these additional capabilities are creating a richer, more engaging learning experience. In addition, the incorporation of these features into a single device allows for a greater breadth of communication options and collaborative learning.

For example, a picture of an error light on a device could save minutes of describing it to a colleague who is helping a field technician troubleshoot and fix a problem. A short video animation of a manual process or procedure could save significant time and reduce errors. A sales professional could make better use of "windshield time" by having Web-based information read back to him or her over a cellular connection, eliminating dangerous visual data access or additional time looking up information upon arrival.

All of these examples point to another trend we have mentioned before: the integration of learning into work. This performance orientation could be the most pervasive and effective use of mLearning technology. The addition of learning elements into mobile applications appears to be one of the most effective areas of early mLearning use, as seen in our case study examples.

eBooks: Electronic Classroom Surrounds Using Wireless Technologies

Have you ever read a book online? Many people start out with a common bias that it is hard to read online, much less learn. This is a fair assumption given the current technical limitations. eBooks currently represent a small emerging trend, but there is considerable potential down the road, particularly in relationship to eLearning.

Let's look at a potential scenario. It's your first day in a university class. You walk in and examine the syllabus. In addition to the lectures and exam sessions that you'll be attending, you note that there is a textbook for the course.

Is the book the course? No, it is a supplement to the course. It is a resource that provides foundational material you can study at your own pace and use as needed to augment the rest of your learning experience in the classroom.

Just as a physical textbook provides that supplement in a real classroom, an eBook can do the same for an eLearning class. There also is great potential to have eBooks do far more than a physical textbook ever could. Let's take a look at the current state of eBook technology and its use and application within eLearning, as well as future trends.

eBooks currently are a nascent part of the overall publishing market. Projected to garner only $251 million of the projected $7.8 billion publishing industry during the next five years, it's easy to understand why eBooks do not capture more attention (O'Brien, 2000).

eBooks can be categorized into several delivery formats. The three main hardware platforms for delivery are: handhelds, specialized devices like the RocketBook, and computer-based readers on a laptop or desktop. Each of these platforms has its own set of characteristics, features, and limitations that are beyond the scope of this book; but suffice it to say that it is still too soon to judge which format will truly take off and meet learner demands.

We're also in the early stages of the technology. One of the biggest drawbacks to any screen-based format is text clarity. Studies have shown that it is 50 percent harder on your eyes to read off of a typical screen compared to paper. Moreover, the same studies show that the average person reads 25 percent slower when reading from a computer when compared to paper. The resolution, along with radiant versus reflective light characteristics, are issues that affect readability and eyestrain. These effects are being addressed through higher resolution pages online, different radiance levels, and technologies like Microsoft ClearType that are greatly improving readability (Bitstream, 2005) http://www.bitstream.com/wireless/index.html.

Another aspect of current eBooks is an artificial linearity (unlike paper-based books) that serves to limit some of the key functions offering superior dynamic content features. Another hindrance is the need to secure the technology from copyright infringements; no one wants a repeat of Napster's effect on the recording industry to occur in publishing. The desire to ensure effective security and commerce infrastructure is a positive, but it also is a hindrance to innovation in other areas. Security needs are limiting the features and open architecture. Secure Digital Rights Management (SDRM) is the dominant security mechanism incorporated into secure eBook readers like those from Microsoft, Adobe, and PalmOne.

Some of the biggest impediments are actually conceptual rather than technical or practical. For instance, eBook means "electronic book" in today's vernacular, but as Pine and Gilmore state, eBook needs to mean "experiential book" (Experience Economy: Harvard BSP, Pine & Gilmore, 1999).

One of the greatest areas of current promise is in the standards-making efforts. The open e-book Forum has come up with a cross-platform specification based on eXtensible Markup Language (XML).

In light of these current issues and trends, let's examine current applications of eBooks to eLearning to see what is currently possible and in use today.

Applications to eLearning

One of the graduate courses that I teach called Internet Management Applications has been using an online eBook format version of Marc Abrams's (1998) popular *World Wide Web: Beyond the Basics*. The book was first published in 1996, but has since been updated. When I first examined the book in both its more recent hardcopy volume and its eBook format, I found that both were a bit outdated for the level of currency I wanted to have in the class. Either one would need to be heavily supplemented with current events, updated statistics, and recent technology innovations. Let's face it: As soon as you write something about the Internet (or on mobile technology for that matter!) it is out of date.

Both the print and digital versions seemed to do a good job covering the core history and necessary background information. I somewhat preferred the hypertext links to outside resources and the chapter flow found in the electronic version, and the online version was offered for free.

I decided to cut my students a break and make the online version required and the paper copy an optional text. Interestingly, since this was the first time many of them had used an eBook, 75 percent of the students decided to buy the paper copy anyway. The response to the eBook, even in a class *about* using Internet technologies in practical applications, was surprising. Some students really liked the format, while others were frustrated that we were not following the flow of the paper-based book. All of this anecdotal information leads to some interesting practices in eBook use for learning.

Future Innovations in eBooks

The e in eBooks will go from meaning "electronic" to "experiential" and eventually "eternal," with rich media integrated to form something that is better than books and continuously up to date (likely via a subscriptions model). We will see formation of communities around cornerstone "books" that provide a point of departure for ongoing exploration and new findings.

There also are implications for linking to courses the same way a text could drive curriculum format, structure, and flow; the eLearning "course" becomes a virtual online workbook supporting the eBook (and vice-versa). You could easily associate texts with courses and make them searchable for easy reference, through establishing a codified system for tracking eBooks based on Resource

Descriptions Framework (RDF) or Learning Object Model (LOM) format (W3C, 2005). This would allow eBooks to be searched and referenced online on a macro scale (consider the Library of Congress online and full-text indexed). Who knows, someday perhaps we will have "The Cosmic Library," much like the "Cosmic Jukebox" underway in music and media (Bielawski & Metcalf, 2005).

Handtop Computing

We're all familiar with the laptop and the PDA, but what's striking is the middle ground that hasn't been fully covered by either platform. Even the more recent tablet PCs don't quite get to the small form factor that many people look for in PDA, combined with the full function capability that one has in a laptop or tablet PC. Enter the handtop computer!

Several devices have started to fill this void. This isn't necessarily a new niche; tools like Intermec devices for the handtop Windows 98 operating system, with a full touch screen and a strap that allows you to hold it in your hand even though it's about two or three pounds, have been around for a while. A new class of devices promises lightweight, smaller form factors and full Windows 2000 or XP operating systems capability, with a touch screen that allows you to use this as a fully functional, handtop device, within the four- to five-inch range and about an inch thick.

It's amazing that this amount of computing power can be put into such a small package with 1 gigahertz (gig) or better processor—full 40-gig hard drives in many cases—a display that's quite usable, and even in some cases, a fold-out keyboard or a slide-out keyboard that's available in the OQO platform (www.oqo.com). Other platforms like the Gazelle allow you to slide a small brick—a desktop synchronization unit—into a handheld player or within a hard drive in conjunction with another computer that's either portable or desktop based.

In addition, there is another genre bleeding into this space with the portable media assistant, or the portable media player—PMP for short. These are players much like the Archos series of devices that allow you to play back video, audio, photo, text, or data files just like you would on a regular hard drive. They can connect to a laptop and be used as a portable drive, even recording video and audio—all in a device that has an LCD screen and anywhere from a 20-gig to a 100-gig hard drive.

Some of the most recent versions also integrate e-mail, Web access, access to contacts and calendars, and even built-in wireless features, along with a gaming engine. They offer a fully integrated mobile device all within just a four- or five-inch framework in terms of physical form factor.

As this new category comes down in price, we are going to see significant use of this in both learning applications as well as personal productivity management and personal knowledge management. I look forward to exploring this unique platform that fills the gap between the two device categories we have been talking about the most within the context of mLearning, and seeing how these new and advanced features can be used in this unique form factor.

Wearable Computers

One step beyond handtop computers, but with a much longer history, is the notion of wearable computing. Since the early days when Dr. Steven Mann was a student tramping around MIT with his belt or backpack wearing computers and headsets with heads-up displays, there's been significant potential for wearable computing (Bass, 1998).

Military groups have seized on this and developed field-based wearable computing for decision and logistical support for commanders in the field and other field-based personnel. This technology has started to trickle down to the consumer market with jackets being marketed with pockets for every mobile device, or with integrated headsets. The result is a product that, combined with your clothing and what you might wear every day, offers you very discreet, wearable computing power at your disposal.

"For example, Nike's ACG COMMJacket, designed for those who like to stay in touch outdoors, features ergonomic wireless communications components combined with a waterproof, breathable outerwear for radio hands-free transmission. Its inside-left chest pocket offers a compact adapter cable that connects to a Motorola two-way radio or compatible mobile phone; once connected, you press the PTT button on the outer storm flap to talk. A collar-high radio speaker on the left shoulder allows you to listen to radio calls without the hassle of headphones or an ear bud, and includes a waterproof microphone to enhance clear transmission. The jacket ships with an instructional CD-ROM." For more information, go to:

http://www.gadgetryblog.com/gadgetryblog/2004/11/nike jacket_has.html

iPods

Another device that has emerged and continues to expand its capabilities is the iPod line. iPod is a class of portable digital audio players designed and marketed by Apple

Computer, as well as by Hewlett-Packard as Apple iPod + HP. The devices offer a simple user interface designed around a central scroll wheel. Most iPod models store media on a built-in hard drive, while the smaller iPod shuffle devices use Flash memory. Like most digital audio players, an iPod can serve as an external data storage device when connected to a computer.

Ron Edwards is President of Ambient Performance, a consultancy helping organizations innovate in learning to get better results from their existing and emerging technologies. Edwards writes of the trend of "Podcasting," a term coined that combines the words *iPod* and *broadcasting.* This involves subscribing to audio content created professionally or otherwise on the device of choice, much like many subscribe to aggregated news feeds. Edwards asserts that while there already is free content available that is of benefit, creating one's own is "quick and easy."

Content, says Edwards, could include audio from business leaders, leadership programs, cultural change-related content, etc., and would be available whether at home, in the car listening to a CD, or on the move with MP3 players, or using cell phones that are increasingly MP3 enabled. The use of portable distributed audio to inform and educate is likely to grow as evidenced by the growing consumer demand for downloadable audio books, he writes. For a more thorough examination of the emerging world of Podcasting, visit:

www.podcastingnews.com and www.podcast.net

In 2004, as part of an experiment, Duke University distributed 20-gig Apple iPod devices to more than 1,600 incoming students. The devices were equipped with Belkin Voice Recorders. The school's Center for instructional

Technology did an evaluation on the academic use of iPods as a tool for faculty and student use, and found positives in the areas of convenience, flexibility, greater student participation, and enhanced support for individual learning preferences and needs. Some drawbacks that were cited included difficulty in integrating multiple systems, locating commercial usage licenses, inherent limitations of the device, and lack of functional knowledge of the iPOD's capabilities among the faculty and students.

Transcoders—LCMSs with Transcoding Functions

Another tool of the future is the transcoder. Transcoding is the process of converting a media file or object from one format to another. Transcoding is often used to convert video formats (i.e., Beta to VHS, VHS to QuickTime, QuickTime to MPEG). It is also used to fit HTML files and graphics files to the unique constraints of mobile devices and other Web-enabled products. Such devices usually have smaller screen sizes, lower memory, and slower bandwidth rates. The transcoding is performed by a transcoding proxy server device, which receives the requested document or file and uses a specified annotation to adapt it to the client. Tools such as IBM's Websphere and Microsoft's ISAPI extensions are toolsets that can automatically transcode content.

Linking to an LCMS (Learning Content Management System) makes it possible to reformat and transform content in real time based on what type of device is requesting the information. If the request comes from a Palm device, the learning material is reformatted for best display on a Palm. While a full exploration of this advanced topic is beyond the scope of this chapter, expect to see much more detail on this topic as the explosion of device types and specialty mobile technology accelerates over time. The only way to address this is through the process of transcoding.

Blogs, Audio Blogs, and the Future of Online Journaling

Blogs—an abbreviation of "Weblogs"—are a unique way to build an infrastructure that can support short journal-style messages that can be delivered to a Web site and updated quickly and easily. It is also possible to easily link one journal to another, connecting blogs to other blogs.

A more recent technology is the audio blog, which involves taking messages that have been presented in audio form, such as MP3, and posting them on the Web for mobile review of the audio content. A whole new category is starting to form around this area, called mBlogs or moBlogs. This technology has significant implications for the production and consumption of content while mobile. It is a more natural way to interact with content while driving in the car or doing something that occupies your visual and motor senses.

Exploring this further, let's consider some late-breaking technology from Nokia. The company is putting together a new software package for some of its most recent mobile devices, handsets, and cell phones. Termed Lifeblogs, the software integrates many of the multimedia elements that a phone is capable of capturing—whether an audio conversation, a short message or text, a video or still image feed from the camera phone portions that are on many of the newest smart phones, or any other type of mixed media—and places these into sort of an online scrapbook or journal that can be played back. This new form of instant digital image capturing or recording is a way to integrate this technology and multimedia with your life—hence the name!

It will be interesting to see if this technology catches on, either from Nokia or other manufacturers that might also pursue this line of digital acquisition in a rapid sort of folksy fashion that allows people to capture expertise and experience—with a minimum amount of the invasion and intrusion that video cameras and other digital technology can often impose. Phones are becoming such a vital part of our overall schema of life when we're traveling and when we're mobile, that it seems likely this will be a key aspect of how mobile information production and consumption will happen in the future.

Mobile Gaming

Along with the trends of mobility in our society, there's also a greater trend toward gaming and the huge business that has grown around online games and console-based games. This trend is starting to bleed into the mobile market now that phones are sophisticated enough to handle rudimentary game logic and deliver out compelling experience. This experiential learning and use of scenarios online holds great promise for teaching both our younger generations and those who grew up playing basic games on anything from a Commodore 64 through Atari and onto Nintendo.

Unlocking the learning and educational uses of these preexisting technologies holds great promise for mobile content delivery. Mobile games is an initial attractor for getting people interested and involved in using mobile performance support and handheld collaboration, and can be part of an effective learning strategy that also includes online courses and traditional face-to-face instruction.

Java is the technology that seems to currently hold the most promise. Flash and Flash Lite from Macromedia are also coming on strong, but with minimum penetration into the handheld market at this point. Recent announcements of their partnerships with Symbian's platform for its 60 series of devices from Nokia and Siemens, and Sony Ericsson and other GM-based phone companies that have incorporated Java into their platform and the Symbian operating system, show an opportunity to combine these technologies and give the best of both worlds.

Under Java, much of the programming logic already exists to build simplified games that are 64k or less, similar to what was possible with the earlier stages of Nintendo. You do, however, have much more control with the devices based on the number of buttons you have on the cellular phone keypad.

J2ME (Java 2 Micro Edition) allows developers to freely access and build modules that can be used on mobile phones, handsets, and other small Java-supported devices. Coupling this with the Web access that many of the current phones have as well as SMS for sending messages, it's very possible to build game logic that can also access content from a centralized Web server. Tying this in with a J2ME game allows you to develop once and deliver on many different platforms. The main issue is that many cell phones don't have the same size screen and button configuration, and often the user interface portion is different. Any game that would be developed needs to be configured many times in order to function on a variety of handheld devices.

In the consumer market, there must be significant economies of scale—thousands of users—in order to be able to make this a worthwhile activity. However, in the corporate market, there are standard employee work packages and a definition of what equipment is available, what handset or PDA might be used, and as an end result, the standard issue from the company. This makes it much more possible to build one version and deliver it out on one unit, and not have to worry about delivering to another type of device until a significant corporate upgrade occurs.

This is where corporations have a significant advantage over both small and medium-size enterprises, as well as over the consumer market for delivery of handheld mLearning content. This particularly applies to games that are more costly to develop than typical course modules, or performance support that's delivered over a handheld unit.

Other engines in addition to Flash and its library of interactive capabilities include the ExEn, WGE, and the Mophun engines, which are seeing their way onto handtop devices and personal media players.

This market is still too new to predict who will be the winner. However, there is significant momentum around the J2ME platform. Flash is a close contender because of its long history on Pocket PCs and recent announcements of integration with newer Symbian devices. Future versions of Flash Lite should be available under not only the Symbian platform, but also the PalmOne platform as well.

Regardless of the technology platform, good learning is not a product of the platform used, but rather the instructional design. If you layer this on top of the engagement needed for good game design, it is a difficult puzzle to put something together that teaches and engages, particularly when there is no other human around. Development of a good game design document (GDD) that encapsulates learning objectives and a purpose beyond the game is a good initial approach for designers to consider.

A few early examples might cast some additional light and direction on how small learning games might be both engaging and effective from a learning perspective. Two examples follow:

BusinessMan

http://www.midlet-review.com/index?content=review&id=24&rel=j2me#supported_handsets

From: Com2Us, www.com2us.com

"This game tests your ability to survive in the cut-throat world of business. COM2US Businessman puts you in the job of handling clients for your company. Adopt strategies for fair trade and keeping your customers loyal. Be careful not to make too many mistakes or you'll find yourself fired and on the streets: game over."

Air Traffic Control

From Lunagames.com

http://www.lunagames.com/game.asp?game=atc

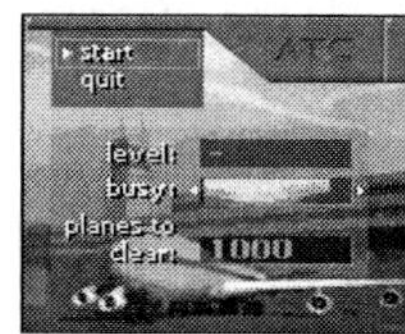

As Lunagames describes their game, you can: "Control the skies above a busy airport as planes enter your airspace. You'll need to lead the planes to their destination and guide the pilots to their final approach so they can land safely.

"The game comes with over 100 levels, practice mode, and an interactive tutorial to help you master the hectic job of Air Traffic Controller."

Games and simulations are a viable way to increase engagement in the content. Understanding the elements of game design can help. A good resource is Richard

Rouse's (2001) *Game Design: Theory and Practice.* Reviewing this material will quickly show that, above the use of media, the element of competition is a key driver to good game design and player (learner) engagement. We look forward to exploring this concept with you further through ongoing dialogue and updates to this material. If you are working in this area, please contact me and let me know what you are doing. I'd love to explore further and share ideas.

Innovative Programs and Projects Academic ADL Co-Lab

So far, most handheld learning applications have been applications ported from the desktop. The Academic Co-Lab, led by Judy Brown, believes that a powerful handheld learning environment might capitalize on the *portability, social interactivity, context sensitivity, connectivity*, and *individuality* of ubiquitous devices to bridge real and virtual worlds. Working with Professor Kurt Squire, the research examines a handheld computer simulation platform designed to exploit the affordability of handheld technologies. With GPS and wireless capability, the platforms enable the development of "augmented reality" simulations, that is, simulations that provide a virtual context layered on top of a real-world context. The handheld computer provides a window into the virtual context that is sensitive to information being supplied to it by the real world. Over the past two years, this platform has been used with nearly 500 high school and college students, as well as with students in informal learning programs through the MIT/Education Arcade's augmented reality gaming platform.

The three applications currently being deployed in Madison, Wisconsin, are:

1. *Environmental Detectives*, an environmental disaster simulation game where players participate in a real-time simulation game based around a toxic contamination in a local watershed. Students must combine real-world (characteristics of the landscape) and virtual-world (virtual readings, interviews with virtual characters) data to identify the cause of the contaminant and design a solution to deal with its effects.
2. *Taken off Campus*, a virtual tour mystery game where players try to uncover the mystery of a rash of burglaries around the UW-Madison campus. Players literally run around the UW campus interviewing characters and investigating landmarks to piece together the puzzle of the stolen valuables. While presented as an entertainment application, this application is designed to explain the history of UW-Madison, share common history and folklore, and enculturate new students into campus life.
3. *A history time travel game* where players virtually travel into the past and into the future to try and reverse the flow of history after a wormhole has appeared and altered Madison history. Players learn about the architecture and history of Madison, including its days as a frontier town, controversies surrounding the late great architect Frank Lloyd Wright, and the controversial riots in Madison in the 1970s.

Although these three applications have differing objectives and different use scenarios, they carry common elements that can be used in any general distance learning application. Specifically, they use *engaging backstory*, *differentiated character roles*, *reactive third parties*, *guided debriefing*, *synthetic activities*, and *embedded recall/replay* to promote both engagement and learning.

Ms. Brown presented the results of an mLearning project sponsored by the European Union. The m-learning.org project, initiated in 2001 and completed last fall, targeted unemployed, underemployed, or homeless youths. These youths were provided with handheld devices that also functioned as phones. A variety of courses such as driving courses and language courses using SMS were administered. The findings of the project were that mLearning helps learners to improve literacy and numerical skills; encourages independent and collaborative learning; helps learners identify areas where they need support; helps combat resistance to use of ICT; removes formality from the learning experience; helps learners remain focused; and raises confidence. Ms. Brown emphasized the significance of a European initiative of recommendations that focused on developing a common core of content to be shared among the countries and ensuring interoperability, open standards, and quality measurements of materials.

MOBIlearn Project

"MOBIlearn is a worldwide European-led research and development project exploring context-sensitive approaches to informal, problem-based and workplace learning by using key advances in mobile technologies.

"The MOBIlearn project consortium involves 24 partners from Europe, Israel, Switzerland, USA and Australia. Their competencies are integrated and extended by a Special Interest Group which includes 250 of the world's leading organisations, active in Information Technology" (MOBIlearn.org, 2005).

Partners include:

Giunti Ricerca S.R. (IT)

University of Birmingham (UK)

Telecom Italia (IT)

Space Hellas S.A. (EL)

Cosmote S.A. (EL)

The Open University (UK)

Emblaze Systems Ltd. (IL)

Deutsche Telekom AG (DE)

University of Koblenz-Landau (DE)

NOKIA Corporation (FI)

University of Zurich (CH)

Stanford University, Center for Design Research (US)

Universitá Cattolica del Sacro Cuore (IT)

Compaq Computer S.R.L. (IT)

SFERA ENEL (IT)

University for Industry (UK)

University of Tampere (FI)

Fraunhofer IFF (DE)

Massachusetts Institute of Technology OKI (US)

Education.au Limited (AU)

Liverpool John Moore University (UK)

Sheffield Hallam University (UK)

Telefónica I+D (ES)

University of Southern Queensland (AU)

While we have made every effort to represent findings and innovations from around the world, this group provides much deeper emphasis on European efforts that have traditionally been ahead of efforts in the United States.

Conclusion

The future is now!

Those in business, education, and the nonprofit and consumer worlds who are open to endless possibilities will help this emerging discipline of mLearning to transform the way people, organizations, and entire communities function. The key is for users at the grassroots level to spread awareness of the time savings, efficiency, and greater results and profits found through the use of such technology in order to fend off skepticism about mLearning while empowering people to become far more productive.

This book has intended to survey, from a corporate perspective, the landscape of how mLearning is being utilized and what lies ahead. Even since this writing, technology, innovations, and ideas have continued to evolve and expand, making the mLearner most certainly a lifelong learner.

Our hope is that you, the reader, will become immersed in this growing universe of innovation—for knowledge is of little use unless it is placed into action! If you have imagined a vision inspired by these chapters about how your life and work can become more seamless, more effective, and even more fulfilling, you owe it to yourself to help that glimpse of tomorrow become a present reality—for yourself and for your learning audience.

References

Abrams, M. (1998). *World Wide Web: Beyond the basics*. New York: Prentice Hall.

Bass, T. A. (1998) Dress code. *Wired Magazine. 6.04*. Retrieved September 22, 2005, from http://www.wired.com/wired/archive/6.04/

Bitstream (2005). Thunderhawk: A wireless web browser from Bitstream. *Bitstream Inc*. Retrieved September 22, 2005, from http://www.bitstream.com/wireless/index.html

Bielawski & Metcalf, D. (2005). *Blended eLearning: integrating knowledge, performance support and online learning. 2nd Edition—Enterprise Class Edition*. Amherst, MA: HRD Press.

Brown, J. (2005, March). *Mobile industry status—where we are and where we are going*. PowerPoint presented at the New Orleans Training 2005 Conference, New Orleans, LA. Retrieved on September 22, 2005, from http://mlearnopedia.com/presentations/MobileIndustry3-1-05

http://www.instat.com/includes_1/home_service_provider_infrastructure.htmGartner Group. (2005). http://www.gartner.com

Jenkins, H., Klopfer, E., Squire, K., & Tan, P. (2004). Look, listen, walk. *Technology Review*. Retrieved September 8, 2005, from http://www.technologyreview.com/articles/04/04/wo_jenkins040204.asp?p=1

In-stat MDR. (2003). http://www.instat.com

Kemp, M. (2005, April). The role of information technology in our lives. *mlearningworld.* Retrieved September 22, 2005, from http://www.mlearningworld.com/index.php?name=Articles&op=show&id=1421

Novak, J. D. (1998). *Learning, creating and using knowledge: Concept maps as facilitative tools in schools and corporations*. Mahwah, NJ: Erlbaum.

O'Brien, D. P. (2000). *Books unbound.* Cambridge, MA: Forrester Research. Retrieved September 22, 2005, from http://www.forrester.com/ER/Research/Report/Summary/0,1338,10088,FF.html

Rouse, R. (2001). *Game design: theory and practice.* Plano, TX: Wordware.

Schrank, D., & Lomax, T. (2002). *The 2002 urban mobility report*. Texas Transportation Institute. Retrieved on September 22, 2005, from http://tti.tamu.edu/documents/ums/mobility_report_2002.pdf

Siebel Systems, Inc. (2005). Why is CRM important? *CRM on Demand.* Retrieved September 22, 2005, from http://www.crmondemand.com/crm/why-is-crm-important.jsp

Spiro, R. J., Coulson, R. L., Feltovich, P. J., & Anderson, D. (1988). Cognitive flexibility theory: Advanced knowledge acquisition in ill-structured domains. In V. Patel (Ed.), *Proceedings of the 10th Annual Conference of the Cognitive Science Society* (pp. 375–383). Hillsdale, NJ: Erlbaum.

Texas Transportation Institute (2002). http://translink.tamu.edu

Veltman, C. (2005, February). Education-to-go is more than an academic matter. *Financial Times*. Retrieved September 22, 2005, from http://news.ft.com/home/us

Webopedia (2005). What is CRM: A definition. *Webopedia Computer Dictionary*. Retrieved September 22, 2005, form http://www.webopedia.com/TERM/C/CRM.html

W3C (2005). W3C: World Wide Web consortium. Retrieved September 22, 2005, from http://www.w3.org/